INTO THEIR SHOES

HELPING THE LOST FIND CHRIST

JOHN KRAMP & ALLEN JACKSON

LIFEWAY
Nashville, Tennessee

TABLE OF CONTENTS

*Thanks to John Kramp for the opportunity
to work with him on this project. He was a
source of inspiration and education.
Creativity is his gift. Thanks to my wife
Judi who is my soul mate, my helpmate,
and my editorial consultant. Thanks to my
children, Aaron and Sarah, who inspire so
many illustrations. Thanks to Chuck Kelley
and the seminary family at New Orleans
Baptist Theological Seminary for affirming
my efforts and to my classes for reality
checks. I pray that students will be
challenged through God's infinite love for
the lost and the found.*

*Allen Jackson
April, 1996*

*John Kramp is Associate Director of
Discipleship and Family Ministries for the
Baptist Sunday School Board in Nashville,
Tennessee.*

*Allen Jackson teaches at New Orleans
Baptist Theological Seminary in New
Orleans, Louisiana.*

INTRO TO LOSTOLOGY

The study of being lost and what that experience
can teach Christians about evangelism.

If you're like most people who are interested enough in evangelism to be reading this book, you're probably an insider—a Christian, active in church, insulated from the secular world by a circle of Christian friends, concerned about lost people but not entirely comfortable in sharing your faith. If that's an accurate description, this book is for you. We who are Christians have our own culture within the walls of our church or church-related ministry. If you've been a Christian for a long time, it may be hard to remember what it's like to be an outsider. If you've grown up in a Christian home and have been in church as long as you can remember, you have no way of knowing what it's like to be an outsider in church.

Lostology is a new field of study, designed to help insiders look at the everyday, real-life experience of being physically lost. Based on that frustrating and sometimes frightening experience, we can begin to understand how lost people feel when they begin a spiritual search for true direction.

MAKING THE MOST OF THIS WORKBOOK

Since your college probably doesn't offer a lostology major, we're plowing new ground. Studying at college is usually more fun with more than one person. The same will be true in your study of lostology. This book includes six chapters; the first is a brief introduction and the last is a practical summary to prepare you to continue living as a certified lostologist. Chapters 2 through 5 focus on six of the laws of lostology. Each chapter includes Bible study, reflection, and application to help you filter the material. After looking at each law, you'll find a Lostology Lab; this is designed for small-group interaction.

If you want even more detail on lostology, *Out of Their Faces and Into Their Shoes*, the book on which this workbook is based, is available in hardcover. The most comprehensive way to study lostology is to read the hardback, work through the workbook, and establish a strategy to apply the principles that you learn throughout the school year.

Welcome to *Lostology 101!*

THE LOSTOLOGY EXPERIENCE

CHAPTER ONE

*This section helps us understand what it's like
to be lost physically
and how that experience
can help Christians understand
spiritually lost people.*

C A S E   S T U D Y

Abigail was driving her car behind the minivan driven by her parents. She had plenty of time to think on the six-hour drive to the university. It was her freshman year, and she was blown away thinking about the newness of the whole deal. New campus. New town. Her home was in a large city, a metropolitan area with museums, sports teams, plenty of malls, and great churches. The university was in a small college town. She had grown up in the same church for most of her life. Now she was going to a new place with new people to start a new phase of her life. She thought about the group of friends that had grown close during her senior year of high school. They knew her and she knew them. She knew what they liked and she even knew how they thought. There was a certain comfort about hanging out with them. Since none of them would attend the same school as Abigail, she would have to meet new people. She knew it was time to spread her wings, but she also knew that there would be different types of people at the university. She had heard that many of them were rich and snobby and couldn't care less about God. She thought to herself, "Will they really be like that? How will they dress? Will they talk funny? How will I fit in? Will I have to keep my faith a secret—will they make fun of me because I'm a Christian? How many other Christians will be around?" ■

REFLECT:

• What advice would you give Abigail if she shared her anxiety with you before she left for college?

_____

_____

_____

APPLY:

• List some of the misconceptions Abigail harbors about students at the university?

1. _____

2. _____

3. _____

4. _____

5. _____

• Why do you think it is so easy for us to generalize about "students at the university" or any other group of people?

_____

_____

_____

The Bible contains an account of a man who left his home for another place. His name was Abraham and his story is found in Genesis 11.

The Lord had said to Abram, "Leave your country, your people and your father's household and go to the land I will show you. I will make you into a great nation and I will bless you; I will make your name great, and you will be a blessing. I will bless those who bless you, and whoever curses you I will curse; and all peoples on earth will be blessed through you." So Abram left, as the Lord had told him; and Lot went with him. Abram was seventy-five years old when he set out from Haran. He took his wife Sarai, his nephew Lot, all the possessions they had accumulated and the people they had acquired in Haran, and they set out for the land of Canaan, and they arrived there" (Gen. 12:1-5).

Abraham's hometown was in a metropolitan city of the ancient world situated on the Euphrates River (in present-day Iraq). It was a commercial crossroads, a cultural capital, and a prosperous center of religion and industry. It was a culture advanced in the fine arts. (Excavations have uncovered beautiful jewelry, crystal, and fine china!) The city came to be known as "Ur of the Chaldees" after the Chaldeans entered southern Babylonia after 1000 B.C. Abraham lived there at its peak.

In sharp contrast, God told Abraham to move to the region along the Mediterranean Sea known as Canaan. Though it was eventually taken and settled by the Jewish people, it was occupied by the warlord Canaanites when Abraham headed there. Canaan stretched from the Jordan River on the east to the Mediterranean Sea on the west. Much of this territory was dry, mountainous, and rocky, unfit for cultivation. It did contain some fertile farmlands, particularly in the river valleys and coastal regions.

About the only thing that Canaan had in common with Ur was that it was situated on the trade routes that stretched from Egypt to Syria and Phoenicia in the north and the ancient Babylonian Empire to the east. This location gave the small region a strategic position in the ancient world. But the significance of that similarity would not be felt until later. Abraham was going to a place that was as new to him as college was to you.

REFLECT:

• What do you and Abraham have in common?

ME   ABRAHAM

_____   _____
_____   _____
_____   _____
_____   _____

• Make a list of the emotions you think Abraham may have felt being in a new place.

_____   _____
_____   _____
_____   _____
_____   _____

Many, if not most, aspects of college are outside of the high school comfort zone. Classes don't meet every day. Professors, unlike high school teachers, may never learn (or care to learn) your name. Dormitory or apartment living presents new challenges. Even if you stay at home, sleeping in the room you have always slept in, it just isn't the same. Some classes are larger than life, with 200 or more people. Some classes are smaller than you'd like (with eight people, there is nowhere to hide if you blow off an assignment!). You face the world for the first time as a young adult.

You are confronted with options. You choose a roommate, you choose your own class schedule, you choose if, where, how, and with whom you will eat. You choose a major (eventually). You choose to study or not to study. You choose your friends. You choose whether to pledge a sorority or fraternity. You are confronted with the reality that your choices matter in ways that they never have before.

You are also bombarded with ideas. Philosophy, western civilization, literature, psychology, economics—your head filled with things from theories to theorems and from rationalization to religion. Virtually every area of your thought life is challenged. Even your ideas about God—no, *especially* your ideas about God—are questioned. Your brain is so quickly fried that you may just want to go home.

APPLY:

• Look at the answers you listed identifying Abraham's feelings. Go back and circle any that also apply to your feelings about starting college.

The result of all the newness of college life is that you may feel less sure about yourself than ever before. It happened to me, too. I had the recurring nightmare that I was late for a class and couldn't remember how to get to the right building. Even if you don't have nightmares, you are at a great place in your life to begin to understand spiritually lost people because the newness of the college environment leaves you feeling a little—well, *lost*. Come on, admit it. You've wandered around the campus without a clue as to where you were. It happens to me all the time (but you need to know that I am one who could be described as "directionally challenged").

Have you felt lost? Lost in the sense that you are supposed to be somewhere and you aren't there? People who are lost in a spiritual sense are lost because they aren't where God is. And to be perfectly honest, evangelizing lost people (or even trying to understand them) was pretty far from my mind when I entered college.

The word "evangelism" conjures up images of confrontation. Christians and non-Christians agree on one thing—they dislike evangelism. No one likes the images of guerrilla missionaries searching the campus for the next convert. Rehearsed questions are machine-gunned at inopportune moments and judgments are made based on the "correct" or "incorrect" responses. Most Christians avoid such gospel showdowns and most non-Christians are glad they do.

APPLY:

• On a scale from 1 to 10, how different were you after a few months in college from your high school identity?

Exactly the same								Dr. Jeckyl & Mr. Hyde	
1	2	3	4	5	6	7	8	9	10

• Were you conscious of choosing who you wanted to be? If so, how?
_____
_____

• How do you feel about evangelism?
_____
_____
_____

• Complete the following statements:
A typical non-Christian is _____
A typical non-Christian likes _____
A typical non-Christian wants _____
A typical non-Christian thinks _____
A typical non-Christian spends time _____
A typical non-Christian spends money _____

12

• How many non-Christians do you know?

    ☐ Some of my best friends are non-Christians.

    ☐ I don't know if any of my friends are non-Christians.

    ☐ I don't know any non-Christians.

    ☐ I'm never in a situation to meet any people who are non-Christians.

    ☐ Everybody I know is a non-Christian.

Most Christians do not understand non-Christians. The temptation on campus is to room with Christians, go to church with Christians, join Christian campus organizations, and have group dates with other Christians. Non-Christian people are not in our loop so we don't know how they feel or what they think, we don't know how to help them. When we do have conversations with them in class or in a study group, we know that they need a personal relationship with Jesus, yet we don't know how to get the conversation started. So we often say nothing. If we really understood spiritually lost people, we could talk about our faith more naturally. Such empathy allows evangelism to be more *in your shoes* than *in your face*—more of a conversation and less of a confrontation. The secret is *lostology*—the study of being lost physically and what that experience can teach Christians about evangelism. That's what this book is about. If we can study biology, psychology, zoology, physiology, we can certainly study lostology. One distinct advantage of the college campus is that other students are open to discussing spiritual things. The university environment is as new to them as it is to you! And while you may not be lost in the spiritual sense, you have been lost in a "directionally-challenged" sense and many of the emotions are similar.

JESUS, THE FIRST LOSTOLOGY MAJOR

In the past, many of us have had a misunderstanding of the word "lost." In the Christian vocabulary, the word lost is the opposite of the word "saved," which is a term used to describe someone who has accepted Jesus' offer of eternal life. The opposite of lost, however, is "found." In describing His mission on earth, Jesus said, *"For the Son of Man came to seek and to save what was lost"* (Luke 19:10). Jesus knew that anyone who would admit to being lost is one with a purpose.

When you say, "I'm lost," you tell the world that there is some place you need to be and you are not there. When you arrived on campus, you probably spent some time looking around. You are exploring, but you are not lost. If you are late for archeology and you cannot find the science building, you are lost. You are supposed to be somewhere and you are not. You will not answer when roll is called. Without a destination, you can say, "I lack direction," but you cannot say, "I'm lost." When someone is supposed to be somewhere and they are not, someone else notices.

By using the word *lost*, Jesus helped us understand the nature of our relationship with God before we became Christians:

• By describing us as "lost," Jesus told us we have spiritual purpose.

From God's perspective, there is a place we should be. God created us to be in a relationship with Him and if we are not with Him, we are spiritually lost.

• By describing us as "lost," Jesus told us we have spiritual value. We are not disposable. God cares that we are not where we should be and values enough to search for us when we are spiritually lost.

When He taught about salvation and evangelism, Jesus told stories about being lost—lost sheep, lost coins, lost sons. He told all three parables in Luke 15. We will look more in depth at these Scriptures later, but for now, notice that in each story Jesus linked lostness with evangelism:

"Suppose one of you has a hundred sheep and loses one of them. Does he not leave the ninety-nine in the open country and go after the lost sheep until he finds it? And when he finds it, he joyfully puts it on his shoulders and goes home. Then he calls his friends and neighbors together and says, 'Rejoice with me; I have found my lost sheep.' I tell you that in the same way there will be more rejoicing in heaven over one sinner who repents than over ninety-nine righteous persons who do not need to repent. Or suppose a woman has ten silver coins and loses one. Doe she not light a lamp, sweep the house and search carefully until she finds it? And when she finds it, she calls her friends and neighbors together and says, 'Rejoice with me; I have found my lost coin.' In the same way, I tell you, there is rejoicing in the presence of the angels of God over one sinner who repents."

"There was a man who had two sons. The younger one said to his father, 'Father, give me my share of the estate.' So he divided his property between them. Not long after that, the younger son got together all he had, set off for a distant country and there squandered his wealth in wild living. After he had spent everything, there was a severe famine in that whole country, and he began to be in need. So he went and hired himself out to a citizen of that country, who sent him to his fields to feed pigs. He longed to fill his stomach with the pods that the pigs were eating, but no one gave him anything. When he came to his senses, he said, 'How many of my father's hired men have food to spare, and here I am starving to death! I will set out and go back to my father and say to him: Father, I have sinned against heaven and against you. I am no longer worthy to be called your son; make me like one of your hired men.' So he got up and went to his father. But while he was still a long way off, his father saw him and was filled with compassion for him; he ran to his son, threw his arms around him and kissed him. The son said to him, 'Father, I have sinned against heaven and against you. I am no longer worthy to be called your son.' But the father said to his servants, 'Quick! Bring the best robe and put it on him. Put a ring on his finger and sandals on his feet. Bring the fattened calf and kill it. Let's have a feast and celebrate. For this son of mine was dead and is alive again; he was lost and is found.' So they began to celebrate.

Jesus made a connection between being lost physically and being lost spiritually. Through these stories and others like them, Jesus helps us to see that He knew (and knows) what lost people feel. He was the first lostologist. He was the first professor of lostology. If He were writing a syllabus for the course, *Principles of Lostology*, it might begin like this:

Upon completion of the course, students should be able to:
- Recall prior experiences of losing valuables and looking for them.

- Identify emotions and information gathered through such experiences.

- Connect those experiences to the way God feels about those on your campus (or work place or home) who are spiritually lost.

- Use the insights gained to shape future behavior and to guide attitudes upon relating to students and faculty who are spiritually lost.

YOU CAN LEARN A LOT BY BEING LOST

CHAPTER TWO

This section helps us understand what's going on with non-Christians before they begin their spiritual search. We often begin with some preconceived notions. Prepare to stretch a little!

THE FIRST 6 LAWS OF LOSTOLOGY
(Lostology 101)

1. BEING LOST CAN BE FUN
2. NO ONE GETS LOST ON PURPOSE
3. GETTING LOST IS EASY
4. YOU CAN BE LOST AND NOT KNOW IT
5. YOU CAN'T FORCE PEOPLE TO ADMIT THAT THEY ARE LOST
6. ADMITTING YOU'RE LOST IS THE FIRST STEP IN THE RIGHT DIRECTION

J onathan was confused. At the beginning of his sopho-
more year, he had pledged a fraternity as a way of
being around non-Christians. He knew that awful
things had been said about the Greek system, but he
also knew that God could use him and that some of
the members of the fraternity would be open to the gospel. He could
make a difference from inside the system. Surely his brothers in the frat
house would eventually see that something needed to change in their
lives and seek a personal relationship with God.

The opposite seemed to be the case. If anything, they were actively
uninterested in the Bible, uninterested in church, and uninterested in
"changing their ways." And sometimes, Jonathan had to admit, it looked
like they were having more fun than he was. Oddly enough, many of
them really didn't seem to know any better. They were polite when spiritual issues came up (and most of them had definite opinions about what
God should be doing with the universe), but whenever the idea of a
personal relationship with Christ surfaced in conversation, Jonathan felt
like he was speaking a foreign language. If Jonathan brought up the
idea that their lives could be missing something, the defense shields
immediately went up. It was as if his fraternity brothers would not admit
that they needed Jesus. Maybe, Jonathan began to think, they don't
even realize it. Maybe they couldn't care less.

Occasionally, Jonathan was tempted to use a "Gospel Gestapo" tactic to confront his fraternity brothers, to bring them to an understanding
that they were playing with fire. They needed to know what was at
stake, but he was afraid that such a tactic would ruin any chance that
he had with his friends, and it never seemed to open any doors anyway.
It would have been easy to get discouraged, but every now and then
(usually when nobody else was around), one of the guys would
approach Jonathan and ask questions. The conversations would start
with meaningless chatter, but eventually turn serious. Jonathan knew
that his friends were beginning to be open to discussions about a relationship with God when he heard at least one statement that began
with, "I have this problem and I don't know anyone else to ask..." ■

REFLECT:

• What assumptions does Jonathan make about fraternity members?

_____

_____

_____

• What do you think about Jonathan's assumptions?

_____

_____

_____

• What would you recommend as the best strategy for sharing his faith in the fraternity house?

_____

_____

_____

• Rank the following words, from most important (1) to least important (5), in helping Jonathan get started in sharing the gospel. Be prepared to defend your ranking.

_____relationship

_____courage

_____knowledge

_____integrity

_____spirituality

APPLY:

• Write a conversation to end the case study. Allow your imagination to let the conversation have several different endings and think about the various endings from the perspective of different characters.

_____

_____

_____

_____

_____

_____

_____

_____

_____

_____

• Identify qualities that made Jonathan approachable.

_____   _____
_____   _____
_____   _____
_____   _____

Lostology Law #1: Being Lost Can Be Fun

Many of us grow up believing that all non-Christians are miserable. We may or may not spend much time around non-Christians and sometimes our understanding of how they think is limited.

REFLECT:
• Test your attitudes. What do you believe about non-Christians?

True or False:

☐ T ☐ F Non-Christians are miserable.

☐ T ☐ F Non-Christians struggle to have meaningful relationships.

☐ T ☐ F Non-Christians try in vain to fill their empty lives with meaning.

☐ T ☐ F Non-Christians fear death and worry about eternity.

What we believe about secular people determines how we attempt to share the gospel with them. While you probably picked up on the exaggerations in the true/false quiz, there was a time when I would have agreed with these statements. Many of the evangelism techniques that I learned on the college campus and in my church assumed that most people believe in God, affirm the authority of the Bible, worry about eternity, and live lives filled with needs that are not being met.

As a result, when I shared my faith, I was like a door-to-door encyclopedia salesman, reciting my canned speech without trying to understand where my "buyer" was coming from. It was a shock to begin to meet people and have friendships with people who were not Christians, but who were not miserable either.

Let's try to understand what it is like to be lost by getting the feel for being physically lost. Imagine that you are on your way to a football game in another town. Your university is playing your archrival. You are in a van with five close friends; you are driving since your uncle loaned you the van. The CD player is blaring with your favorite group; the ice chest is full of soft

19

drinks. You have plenty of food for tailgating and it is a beautiful fall afternoon. You haven't seen a road sign in a while, and slowly you realize that you have no clue where you are. You announce that you may have missed a turn (or five) and you haven't the slightest idea which direction to go. Oddly, no one seems to mind. You are lost, but you are having fun anyway.

APPLY:

• Recall a time when you had a pretty good time being lost.

_____

_____

_____

• What would you have missed if you had not been lost?

_____

_____

_____

Let's look at the first part of the story of the lost son from Luke 15:

Jesus continued: "There was a man who had two sons. The younger one said to his father, 'Father, give me my share of the estate.' So he divided his property between them. Not long after that, the younger son got together all he had, set off for a distant country and there squandered his wealth in wild living."

Jesus described the fun side of being lost. The younger son had time on his hands, money in his pockets, and adventure on his mind. His only agenda was to get away from home—as far away from home as possible—and to make it on his own. You know some people who came to college with exactly the attitude that Jesus described. You may even have been one of those people. If you had asked the younger son if he was lost, he probably would have replied, "If this is lost, I'm loving it!"

The Bible never said that sin isn't fun. It does help, however, to understand that the fun doesn't go on forever. Remember the next part of the parable:

After he had spent everything, there was a severe famine in that whole country, and he began to be in need. So he went and hired himself out to a citizen of that country, who sent him to his fields to feed pigs. He longed to fill his stomach with the pods that the pigs were eating, but no one gave him anything. When he came to his senses, he said, 'How many of my father's hired men have food to spare, and here I am starving to death!

REFLECT:

• Read Proverbs 10:23. Rewrite it in your own words.

_____

_____

_____

- Rewrite the story for your campus newspaper using this headline—

COLLEGE STUDENT FORFEITS SCHOLARSHIP; SQUANDERED WEALTH IN WILD LIVING.

_____
_____
_____
_____
_____
_____
_____
_____
_____
_____
_____
_____
_____
_____
_____

The truth is that people can have fun being lost. I don't know about you, but I sometimes grow impatient with people who are walking on the wild side. But ponder this wonderful mystery: Those are the very people who liked having Jesus around! And Jesus liked being with them. He seemed to be there at just the exact moment when they realized that something was missing.

APPLY:
- Look up the following Scriptures and identify:
  (1) the lifestyle that the person was living
  (2) the signal that he or she was ready to talk about spiritual direction

- _Luke 5:27-32_
  (1) _____
  (2) _____

- _Luke 7:36-39_
  (1) _____
  (2) _____

- _John 4:7-29_
  (1) _____
  (2) _____

- _John 8:1-11_
  (1) _____
  (2) _____

Remember that Jesus was the first lostologist. Lostologists understand that eventually those same party people will have needs that surface—questions about life, anger about tragedy, grief over death that has struck too close to home. These are opportunities for sharing the faith story. In a television studio, when the red light is on, the camera is receiving everything in the path of its lens. When a non-Christian has questions, the red light is on and Christians must be there to send some positive directions to find the way home.

Remember that one of the most effective things you can do in evangelism is ask a good question and then listen. Here are some questions you can use to get a conversation started about spiritual things:

- Why do you think you are on this planet?
- What is your memory of religion growing up?
- Does your religion help you answer the important questions you are asking about life?
- Does it explain why you are here?
- What are the questions you are asking?

REFLECT:

- What questions would you add to the list above?

_____

_____

_____

- With a Christian friend role-play the possible answers that a secular person might give to the questions above. (Remember to take turns and keep in mind the emotions you experienced when you were physically lost.)

LOSTOLOGY LAB

- Discuss times when you tried to share your faith with someone who was in the "lost-but-loving-it" stage. How did you feel?

_____

_____

_____

_____

_____

_____

- Have you ever met someone who was not responsive to the gospel, but circumstances changed his or her mind? Explain the change in circumstances and attitude.

_____

_____

_____

_____

_____

LOSTOLOGY LAW #2: NO ONE GETS LOST ON PURPOSE

I heard recently of a college prank in which some construction technology students sneaked into a faculty building at night and walled the entrance to the office of a favorite professor. They removed the door, framed the opening, hung the plaster board, painted the new wall the same color as the rest of the hallway, and escaped with time to spare so the paint could dry before morning. Where there used to be a door with the professor's nameplate on it, there was now a wall that looked just like the rest of the hallway.

Can you imagine the innocent teacher who has not yet had his first cup of coffee staring at a section of wall where his office used to be? Confused, perhaps a bit disoriented—*I think I'm in the right place, but this doesn't look familiar…*

Perhaps you've had a similar feeling. For the first time, you have a class in a particular building on campus. You enter this new building with no sense of where you are. When you think you've finally located the room listed on your schedule, no one looks even vaguely familiar. You wait with a knot in your stomach for the professor to announce the class before you unload your backpack. Slowly it dawns on you that you're in the wrong room, but you're not sure where you made a wrong turn.

If you can recall a similar situation, ask yourself this question: Did you get lost on purpose?

No! Of course not. Although many of us frequently get lost, we always have a good excuse—reason—for getting lost.

Jesus understood people who were spiritually lost. He knew that they were not lost on purpose. Every conversation Jesus had with spiritually lost people reveals that He had not written them off as terminally lost. To a tax collector, He said, *"Zaccheus, come down immediately. I must stay at your house today"* (Luke 19:5). Zaccheus didn't mean to be lost, he just was. How did he get that way?

REFLECT:
• Write a diary entry in which Zaccheus tries to describe how he came to be like he was before he met Jesus.

Zaccheus

_____
_____
_____
_____
_____
_____

Remember the parables of lost things from Luke 15? In each of the parables, the lost things did not get lost deliberately. The lost sheep didn't mean to be lost; it simple nibbled its way away from the flock. The coin did nothing to cause it to be lost, but was lost due to the carelessness of someone else. Even the rebellious son who left home became lost as he gradually made bad choices followed by more bad choices. He was responsible for his actions but did not intend to end up in a pig pen!

APPLY:

• Try to come up with a modern version of each parable:
   • Who would be a "lost sheep" on your campus? How could he or she have nibbled away from the flock?

_____

_____

   • Who could be symbolized by the "lost coin"? How did other people contribute to his or her getting lost?

_____

_____

   • Who is the "lost son"?

_____

_____

It's possible that you can see the men and women in your classes, dorms, sororities, labs, and clubs in these parables. Some students intend to check out who God is, but just never get around to it. They are sheep who have nibbled further and further away from where they need to be. Some of them are people who grew up in secular homes without the opportunity to go to Sunday School, participate in a church youth group, or even hear the gospel. They are coins, lost by someone else. Maybe they are sons and daughters who left home thinking that they had all the answers only to find their questions multiplied. They miscalculated the resources they would need to live life and ended up bankrupt. But they didn't mean to.

LOSTOLOGY LAB

• How would you start a conversation about spiritual things with someone on your campus who is too busy for God?

_____

_____

_____

_____

• Have you spoken to a person who grew up in a non-Christian home and never attended church? How did he respond when you began talking with him about a relationship with Christ?

_____
_____
_____
_____

• Are there people on your campus who have miscalculated the resources they need to get through life? How does this influence what you tell them about God?

_____
_____
_____
_____

LOSTOLOGY LAW #3: IT IS EASY TO GET LOST

See if this scenario hits close to home. You are in a class—let's say, accounting. You know that the worksheets must be done more or less daily in order to stay up with the material. Then one day, a basketball game comes up. Then, a concert. After that, a student government meeting. A date. Before you know it, you have a pile of accounting worksheets and not enough days left to catch up with the class. It's easy to fall behind.

You have to work to avoid getting behind in your classes. The same thing is true about getting lost. Do nothing special and you will get lost every time. Lost happens. Lost is life's default mode.

REFLECT:
• List 10 things that are easy to do—things that will happen automatically if you simply do nothing.

1. _____   6. _____
2. _____   7. _____
3. _____   8. _____
4. _____   9. _____
5. _____   10 _____

• Why is it so easy to get lost physically?

_____
_____

• How does this help us empathize with those who are lost spiritually?

_____
_____
_____

Spiritually lost people are lost because it is easy to drift away from God. Like sheep who graze their way to the other side of the pasture, spiritually lost people may not realize what they are doing. It's easy to be lost.

Empathy based on what it feels like to be lost when we didn't plan otherwise helps us guard against judging lost people too harshly. A typical non-Christian student might be confused spiritually for a number of reasons:

- decisions made by his parents about lifestyle and church involvement
- the influence of the friends he hung around with in junior and senior high school
- consideration of what it will take to succeed in his intended major and career
- traditions in the community where he grew up (A church youth group may not have been an option.)

Many college students are lost because they didn't make plans not to be lost, but it is easy to be lost. Awareness of this basic principle of lostology can serve as a reminder to be patient.

APPLY:

• Play the word association game. Write down the first thing that comes to mind when you think of spiritually lost people with regard to:

beliefs about God _____

vocabulary _____

moral preferences _____

things they have done in the past _____

• Brainstorm two sets of responses to each of the possibilities that you identified in the word association game. First, write your instinctive response. Then write a response that a lostologist might give.

(1)_____
_____
_____

(2)_____
_____
_____

It is helpful to recall that before God's intervention in our lives, we were just as likely to have weird beliefs about God, equally capable of using profanity, and very possibly bent toward lifestyle choices that would not make the religious "hall of fame." When we allow our lives to intersect with lost people without putting them down, we place ourselves in a position to answers the questions they will eventually ask.

LOSTOLOGY LAB

• How do you respond when non-Christians tell you what they believe? As a lostologist, what will change about how you talk with secular people?

_____

_____

• How do you feel about the behavior of non-Christian students?

☐ I am sometimes shocked.

☐ I am quick to judge.

☐ I want to share "I was bad, too" stories.

☐ I _____.

• What would Jesus do?

_____

_____

_____

LOSTOLOGY LAW #4: YOU CAN BE LOST AND NOT KNOW IT

Between my senior year in high school and my freshman year in college, I drove toward Dallas to visit my grandmother. There was some construction in progress on the interstate, and I needed gas anyway, so I decided to exit. I thought of the single lane of traffic on the interstate, driving 30 miles per hour alongside orange cones. I did what any freshman would do. I decided I could find a better way.

Though I did not know it at the time, from the moment that my brain processed the possibility of a short cut, I was lost. I drove merrily along, convinced that the interstate would reappear just over the next hill. The more I drove, the more lost I became. I began to sing, "I love to drive and it shows..." Finally, I did the unthinkable. I stopped at a convenience store to ask for directions. (This was a major blow to my pride.) I had been driving in the opposite direction. I was lost, but I thought I was right on track.

APPLY:
• Many of the people Jesus encountered believed they were heading in the right direction, but they were lost. Read Matthew 19:16-30.

• Where did the rich young man think he was headed?

_____

_____

• What did Jesus say to help him realize that he was lost?

_____

_____

The young man misunderstood who Jesus was and what He came to do. He was headed in a wrong direction and didn't realize it. Still, Jesus did not become impatient or get in his face in a confrontation. He wasn't always so soft-spoken, but here He modeled how to be ready with good directions.

Remember that if we are to help secular people understand that they are on the wrong road (or traveling in the opposite direction from where they should be), we have to continually check the map ourselves.

LOSTOLOGY LAB

• Think of a time when you were lost physically but didn't know it? Focusing on that experience—how it happened and how you felt—can help you empathize with non-Christians who are spiritually lost and are unaware of their own condition. Reflect on these questions:

• What factors caused you to believe you were going in the right direction?

_____

_____

_____

_____

• How far did you go before you knew you were lost?

  ☐ less than a mile

  ☐ a couple of miles

  ☐ farther than I'm willing to admit

• While you were lost, did you remain confident that you were going in the right direction?   ☐ yes   ☐ no

• What began to make you think you were going in the wrong direction?

_____

_____

_____

_____

28

LOSTOLOGY LAW #5:
YOU CAN'T FORCE PEOPLE TO ADMIT THAT THEY ARE LOST

My wife calls it "the guy thing." For some reason, the male chromosome contains a set of genetic wires that do not allow us to readily admit that we are lost. When I am driving with other people in the car, I am thoroughly irritated when someone has the audacity to confuse the situation with facts, by coming right out and saying, "You're lost, aren't you?" Folks think they are so smart, just because they are starting to recognize—-no, memorize—the scenery (we learn by repetition).

When we are lost, we hate to admit it. And, we can't force someone to admit he is lost.

REFLECT:
• Identify the top three things that you hate to admit:

(1)_____

(2)_____

(3)_____

• Why is it that we aren't comfortable admitting that we are lost?

_____

_____

_____

• If you were driving and you suspected you were lost, but didn't know for sure, how would you respond to the "You're lost, aren't you?" accusation from your passenger? List three responses.

(1)_____

(2)_____

(3)_____

• Name at least one person who would not hurt your feelings if he or she challenged your directions._____

• Why do you respond differently to this person than to others?

_____

_____

When I am lost, I try to hide the fact that I am clueless regarding directions. My wife, however, is on to this game. If I am quiet for a while and casually ask, "Honey, did you see a sign for Highway 55?" she immediately begins to suspect that I don't know where I am or where I am going. So, she will subtly ask, "Are we taking the scenic route again?" The female chromosome contains some part that enables her to especially treasure and enjoy these moments.

"No, we aren't taking the scenic route, again. I am—uh—looking for a place to stop in case the kids need to go to the restroom."

Then she plays her trump card: *The kids are at Grandma's for the weekend.* I hate to admit that I am lost.

We simply do not want to admit that we are not where we need to be, and it's like a slap in the face when others suggest that we're lost. They are questioning our competence. Just because we are temporarily directionally challenged, we don't want it to be common knowledge among the masses.

As lostologists, we know that people can be lost and not know it. But simply announcing, "Hey, buddy, you're lost. Admit it." won't get us anywhere. First, Buddy probably didn't ask for our evaluation and therefore, he isn't ready to know that he's lost (see law #4). Second, even if he has an inkling that you could be right, he has to admit that he's wrong and it's unlikely that he will admit it in a confrontational approach.

APPLY:

• You are in the car with someone who is obviously lost. Suggest a lead-in sentence to gently remind the directionally-challenged person that it would be futile to continue on the present course.

_____

_____

_____

• Now write the opposite. Be as abrupt as you want to. Tell the driver that he is lost.

_____

_____

_____

• How would you expect the responses to change with each approach?

_____

_____

_____

Jesus constantly dealt with people who didn't want to admit that they were lost. Especially significant were His encounters with the religious leaders of the day. He took the lead from His cousin John in dealing with the Pharisees. Look up Matthew 3:1-8. Notice John's refusal to baptize the Pharisees and Sadducees. Talk about pointing out someone's lostness! Jesus took a similar track in Matthew 23. Check that out now as well.

In college, I heard a lot about "apologetics," the discipline where we logically and passionately defend our faith. Through exhaustive study, one breaks down the explanations that some scientists and philosophers have attempted to provide for the mysteries of God. I loved apologetics. I would often subscribe to the idea that if I knew enough about God, then I could argue someone into accepting Christ. I studied possible objections to my presentation. I was ready with counterstrikes when they would try to resist. Guess what? I didn't have any converts. Don't get me wrong. Apologetics is a worthy field, and believers should exercise their minds to the fullest. It is entirely appropriate to investigate the claims of Christ and to challenge the world's erroneous explanations of God-events. My problem was that I sometimes became more interested in winning the argument than winning the person to Christ.

We need to be ready with a clear explanation of what Jesus has done in our lives. We also can understand through lostology that people who are ready to argue aren't ready to admit that they are lost. And they aren't ready to be found until they can admit they are lost.

REFLECT:

• Have you ever won an argument and damaged a relationship in the process? Which is more important, the relationship or the satisfaction of knowing you were right?

_____

_____

_____

_____

APPLY:

• Consider the following verses which instruct us to be ready to explain our faith:

But in your hearts set apart Christ as Lord. Always be prepared to give an answer to everyone who asks you to give the reason for the hope that you have. But do this with gentleness and respect (1 Pet. 3:15).

Don't have anything to do with foolish and stupid arguments, because you know they produce quarrels. And the Lord's servant must not quarrel; instead, he must be kind to everyone, able to teach, not resentful. Those who oppose him he must gently instruct, in the hope that God will grant them repentance leading them to a knowledge of the truth, and that they will come to their senses and escape from the trap of the devil, who has taken them captive to do his will (2 Tim. 2:23-26).

• What is the aim of such a conversation?

_____

_____

_____

While we cannot argue or coerce people into admitting that they are lost, we can try to raise questions in their minds about their spiritual condition. Many non-Christians on your campus are overly optimistic about their relationship with God. They may be relying on the faith of their parents or the fact that they occasionally attended church when they were young. More common is the belief that as long as they aren't as bad as some other person, then they will get by in God's eyes. After all, doesn't He grade on the curve?

It may help to give non-Christians a frame of reference. Bill Hybels uses the following illustration. Draw a ladder on a piece of paper and explain that it represents the way we move toward God. God is at the top; people are at the bottom. Ask those you are talking with where they think they are on the ladder.

Before they respond, give them a strong dose of perspective. Explain that if Billy Graham or Mother Teresa or any other famous spiritual person were asked where they ranked apart from Jesus Christ, these leaders would put themselves on one of the lower rungs. Then show them that you would place yourself even below those folks. Pause for a moment and ask again where they think they would be. It is usually quite an adjustment for most people. For secular people it may help raise enough questions about their relationship with God to start a conversation.

When Jesus was dealing with spiritual insiders, He confronted them directly. When He was speaking to spiritual outsiders, He illustrated their lostness through stories and parables. His stories contained powerful metaphors that did not allow the listeners to walk away without being affected. They didn't always become believers, but they always had plenty to think about.

LOSTOLOGY LAB

• Think about the non-Christians that you know on campus (or at home). How did they respond once they learned what the Bible teaches about salvation and the fact that those without Christ are spiritually lost? Did they welcome the message or resist? Why?

_____
_____
_____
_____
_____

• Have you ever tried to force someone to admit he or she was spiritually lost? Explain what happened.

_____
_____
_____
_____
_____

32

I have to admit that it bothers me when drivers in other cars seem to be doing everything except driving. At speeds that only begin at the legal limit, men are reading the morning newspaper. Women are applying nail polish. Many people are eating or drinking. Every other person is talking on the phone. It drives me nuts.

There is one exception. When I see someone who has a map spread out over the steering wheel, I have the sudden, compassionate urge to roll down my window and offer assistance. I want to say, "Where do you want to be? I will be glad to take you there." There is something about a traveler who obviously needs help that makes me want to stop.

REFLECT:

• When you have a growing realization that you are lost as you drive down the road, would you stop and ask directions or keep driving?

☐ I'd stop.

☐ I'd keep driving.

What factors would go into your decision?

☐ schedule

☐ purpose of trip

☐ traveling companions

☐ destination

☐ other

• Recall a time when you pulled out a road map only after you were lost. Rate your frustration level at the time by circling a number below.

calm as a cucumber							ready to blow my stack		
1	2	3	4	5	6	7	8	9	10

• If someone actually did stop and offer help while you had the map out, how would you respond?

_____

_____

As humbling as it is to admit that we are lost, it is the first step in turning around to go in the right direction. We must swallow our pride. We must admit defeat. We must begin mental preparations for the inevitable. We were almost right. (Or we were approaching another galaxy we were so lost.) At any rate, at some point we admit that we no longer have a clue.

Let's say that I finally pull into a store to ask the cashier for directions. Did I admit I was lost when I actually asked for directions? No, I admitted I was lost when I pulled the car off of the road to ponder whether or not I wanted to drive back two miles to the last evidence of electricity that I was likely to see for awhile.

When Jesus told the story of the prodigal son, He described the young man's experience as he moved out on his own, lived the "fast life" on his family inheritance, and ultimately ended up feeding pigs when he ran out of funds. (The financial aid office must have been closed.) That young man, standing among the pigs, grew so hungry that he began to look with longing at the slop the pigs ate. For him, that longing was the jolt which shocked him into a decision. He admitted he was officially lost.

Jesus described that moment in the young man's life as the time that he "came to his senses." How appropriate. Out of the confusion, he finally made a decision. He pulled over and scanned the map out to attempt to see where he got off track. His life situation was screaming that he was not in a place where he intended to be, needed to be, or wanted to be. In our churches or in meetings in Christian organizations on campus, we often allow persons the opportunity to respond. When somebody does raise his hand, fill out a card, or talk to a counselor, he is finally admitting that he is lost.

APPLY:

• How much of a struggle is it to admit that you are lost? From "not hard at all" to "ultimate difficulty," circle where you rank in the process of admitting that you need help for life direction.

Can You Admit That You Are Lost?

1	2	3	4	5	6	7	8	9
It's not hard at all.		I need a little help with this step.		I'm in over my head.		I can't do this no matter what.		This is the ultimate difficulty for me.

Evangelism becomes less threatening when we are encouraged by signs that people on our campus are studying the map. Directions are sought, a first step to admitting lostness. Lostologists learn to watch for signs that people are beginning to admit they are lost. Here are a few indicators:

- an interest in reading the Bible or Christian literature
- a question about the existence of God or what Christians believe
- an interest in attending church or a meeting of a Christian organization on campus
- coming into your room in no apparent hurry to "just talk"
- regrets over decisions made in the past

There are still many others who are not ready to admit they're lost. We can pray for them. We can continue to have a quiet faith that shows Jesus is a valid person to know in daily situations. But we don't have to push. Certainly, we care about the eternity of the person sitting next to us in class or at work, but we are confident that God will do His work in His time.

LOSTOLOGY LAB

• Imagine that you are traveling an interstate highway on your way to an important meeting. Unfortunately, you missed a turn and you have been traveling in the wrong direction. Gradually you begin to wonder if you are going in the right direction; things don't "feel right." A sign indicates you are one mile from an exit where you can ask directions. A smaller sign indicates that if you do not take this exit, you will have to continue for 27 more miles to the next exit.

You pull off the highway to look at your map. You have not changed direction, but at least you are no longer moving further away from where you need to be. In what ways do non-Christians make a "pull-off-the-road-and-think-about-it" decision concerning their spiritual lives? How is this different from admitting they are spiritually lost? How is this different from asking for spiritual directions?

_____
_____
_____

• While looking at your map, you say to yourself, "I don't know how this happened, but I'm not where I'm supposed to be. I'm not where I thought I was after all this time. I'm lost." What is the value of that admission? What are the consequences of that admission?

_____
_____
_____

Congratulations! You passed Lostology 101!
Now you can move onto Lostology 201.

WHEN ALL ELSE FAILS, ASK DIRECTIONS

CHAPTER THREE

This chapter helps us to focus on how we give spiritual directions to people who have begun a spiritual search. Consider your lost friends who have "pulled off the side of the road." They may not be ready to be found, but they are trying to figure out how to continue the journey. They have begun to ask. Prepare to be challenged concerning all of the things that you take for granted!

THE SECOND 6 LAWS OF LOSTOLOGY
(Lostology 201)

7. WHEN YOU'RE LOST, YOU'RE OUT OF CONTROL

8. JUST BECAUSE YOU'RE LOST DOESN'T MEAN YOU'RE STUPID

9. IT'S TOUGH TO TRUST A STRANGER

10. PEOPLE ASK FOR DIRECTIONS WITHOUT REVEALING THEIR TRUE EMOTIONS

11. DIRECTIONS ARE ALWAYS CONFUSING

12. UNNECESSARY DETAILS MAKE DIRECTIONS MORE CONFUSING

aron was beginning to wonder why he had agreed to drive. As a management major, he had taken several courses dealing with leadership, administration, and working with people. But nothing in his studies had prepared him for this. He was becoming more and more frustrated as he tried to navigate in a strange place. He looked desperately for landmarks—something—anything—that would get him back on track. He saw nothing familiar.

Eighteen students were attending a national conference in a large city 600 miles from campus. A week before the trip, one of the adult drivers had to cancel. Aaron was asked to drive the second van. There was nothing very spiritual about it—they needed someone over 21 years of age. Aaron agreed. He and the leader met to plan routes and map out details for travel. It seemed like such a good idea at the time.

As the caravan arrived in the metropolitan area excitement began to peak. Aaron smiled as he listened to the chatter coming from the rear seats. Waiting for a light to change, he looked in the rear view mirror and smiled. The students were young and full of promise. When the light changed, he did not see the other van. He wasn't worried—they probably turned somewhere while Aaron was at the light. Sixteen blocks later, the other van was nowhere to be seen. Now he was worried.

The city seemed huge and the map appeared to be printed in Egyptian. Aaron was lost, but he was hesitant to stop for directions—for several reasons. He wanted to keep moving in case the other van was waiting somewhere. He was uneasy about stopping in a place where he knew no one, and he didn't want the others to think that he didn't know what he was doing.

When he saw a friendly looking pedestrian, Aaron rolled down his window and casually asked, "Is this the way to the convention center?" She looked puzzled momentarily before offering directions: "Gotothenextlightormaybethenextandgosouthonabigwidestreetandgotil youseetheoldSearsstoreafterthatgotwoorthreeblockstilyouhitMainandther eyouare."

Aaron admitted the inevitable. He was lost enough to tell the group and to stop for some real directions.■

REFLECT:
• Add to the list as many of Aaron's emotions as you can imagine. Beside each one, write a sentence telling of a time when you felt that way when you were physically lost.

fear _____

frustration _____

_____ _____

_____ _____

_____ _____

• Who do you trust when you are lost? Why or why not?

☐ a police officer _____

☐ a taxi driver _____

☐ a pedestrian _____

☐ any official looking person _____

☐ _____ _____

• What is the main factor that would cause you to stop and ask directions if you were lost?

_____
_____
_____

APPLY:
• Some directions are "good" directions and some are "bad" directions. List 10 qualities of "good" directions.

1. _____ 6. _____

2. _____ 7. _____

3. _____ 8. _____

4. _____ 9. _____

5. _____ 10. _____

• Write out some of the reasons that Aaron may have given for getting lost.

_____

_____

_____

_____

LOSTOLOGY LAW #7:
WHEN YOU ARE LOST, YOU ARE OUT OF CONTROL

Anyone who has ever been responsible for other people can identify with Aaron. We've all been lost. Sometimes it can be fun. More often, it is miserable. Why do we dislike that emotion so much? Think back. What did you fear? Why did you hesitate to ask directions?

The scariest thing about being lost is that we are out of control and that's not a feeling we enjoy. We like to be in control of our lives. We want to drive our own cars, listen to our own music, follow our own schedule. Then a class you want is closed during registration. Two important meetings are scheduled for the same time. You're not in control of your time. Options disappear when you are out of control.

Remember the prodigal son? The ultimate college freshman went away with multiple friends and multiple options—made possible by a pocket with multiple dollars.

"Not long after that, the younger son got together all he had, set off for a distant country and there squandered his wealth in wild living. After he had spent everything, there was a severe famine in that whole country, and he began to be in need" (Luke 15:13-14).

Whatever wild living was, it was expensive. When his inheritance was gone (as well as his drinking buddies), the lost young man reached the point where he had no options except to go home. His options went the way of his money and friends. With the decision to go home, the young man gave up control of his life. He became vulnerable. He could not choose how his father would respond. As a matter of fact, he envisioned a future as one of his father's hired hands with rules much stricter than when he lived at home before.

REFLECT:
• Describe a time when your plans didn't turn out like they were supposed to. What went wrong? How did you feel and respond when you "lost control" of your options?

_____

_____

_____

_____

In talking with campus ministers from various colleges, I discovered that their descriptions of students who come to a ministry event for the first time are remarkably similar. Initially these newcomers visit with a friend who is outgoing. They let their friend do the talking, they avoid eye contact during introductions, they sit near the back of the room, and often leave before the meeting is over. If the event is away from a familiar campus location, their behavior suggests that they are even more nervous.

Students who just happen to walk into the building are usually alone. They pause at the door, glance around as if they are looking for someone, make a loop through the place, and head out the door. If someone engages them in conversation, they usually indicate that they were just looking for a phone. They are attempting to control as much of their environment as possible. For students who haven't been involved in church, any contact with Christians can be intimidating. They are looking for something, or they wouldn't bother, but they don't want to admit that they need anything.

APPLY:

• Make a "Top 10" list of the responses that you have heard (or said!) in conversations with people who are visiting a church or ministry setting for the first time. Consider answers to the question, "What brings you here?"

1. _____

2. _____

3. _____

4. _____

5. _____

6. _____

7. _____

8. _____

9. _____

10. _____

• How can your experience of being "out of control" make you more sensitive to a student who comes to your groups or church for the first time?

_____

_____

_____

_____

We who are Christians must remember what it is like to be lost and out of control. Consider these pointers when you invite secular students to attend church or campus meetings with you:

• Allow them to be anonymous spectators if they want. Don't pull them around frantically introducing them to all of your friends.

• Give them the opportunity to tell their story in small installments. As trust grows, they will share more of their hurts or needs with you.

• Anticipate situations that will make them stand out in the crowd. Help them fill out guest cards assuring them that doing so will not bring an army of zealous people to their dorm room for "follow up."

Remember how you have felt when you were "out of control." Do for others what you wish people had done for you!

LOSTOLOGY LAB

• Which character most accurately describes you when you're lost? Elaborate on your personal strategy for compensating for the loss of control when you are lost:

MY CHARACTER   **WHY I RESPOND THIS WAY**

☐ Billy Belligerent _____

☐ Myra Martyr _____

☐ Ernie Escape _____

☐ Dolly Denial _____

• Imagine that you have been invited by a friend to attend a meeting of another religious group on campus. You have heard the word "cult" used to describe the group.

Would you simply decline or attend out of respect and curiosity?
    Why? _____
_____

Would you go with your friend or would you prefer to meet him there?
    Why? _____
_____

Would you want to wear a name tag?
    ☐ yes ☐ no Why? _____
_____

Would you want to stand and introduce yourself to the group?
    ☐ yes ☐ no Why? _____
_____

Would you want to sing the songs that the group used in the meetings?
☐ yes ☐ no Why? _____
_____

Would you fill out a registration card?
☐ yes ☐ no Why? _____
_____

• Does it help to put yourself into the other person's shoes to see how it feels to be an outsider in a group of well-organized, well-intentioned strangers? Identify the feelings you would experience.

☐ I would feel intimidated.   ☐ I would feel a little bit scared.

☐ I would feel angry.   ☐ I would feel manipulated.

☐ I would feel welcomed.   ☐ I would feel overwhelmed.

☐ I would feel _____.   ☐ I would feel _____.

• Why would you feel these emotions?
_____
_____
_____

• What could you do differently next time you invite someone to attend a church or ministry meeting with you?
_____
_____

LOSTOLOGY LAW #8: JUST BECAUSE YOU'RE LOST DOESN'T MEAN YOU'RE STUPID

One of the jobs that comes rather naturally for youth ministers is that of bus/van driver. Driving a bus has its high points and low points. Lowest of low is when you get lost: you are so sure that you know exactly where you're going and *poof*, something happens. *Clueless in Cleveland.* You know that the place you want to go is so close you can smell it—but your nose is suddenly stopped up. The air conditioner cannot begin to cool the vehicle enough as beads of sweat appear on your forehead, upper lip, and palms. Feelings of responsibility overwhelm you. The "what if?" game kicks in. *What if I am in the wrong city (variations include wrong state, wrong country, wrong planet, etc.)? What if I miss the concert completely? What if I drive around so long that they give our hotel reservations away? What if I am unable to deliver this precious cargo back to their unsuspecting families?*

As the "what if?" game runs its course, you begin thinking about how to cover the fact that you are lost. One of the worst things about being lost is that a devious plan will inevitably unfold. The conspirators are your no-longer-unsuspecting passengers and anyone who might give you directions. The plan has a simple goal: to make you feel as stupid as possible. Fourteen junior highers say things like, "My dad gets lost too, but he's *old*," or "Even I would know how to get there if I was driving."

Then there are the potential direction givers. They eye you with suspicion and a snide half-snicker as if to say, "He's lost, and he's stupid too!" Some direction givers enjoy the power that comes with knowing something that you don't—"You'll have to wait until I defrost the freezer in the back of the store." Or, "I'll help you as soon as I rebuild the engine on this car." I'm kidding—sort of. In most cases, direction givers don't intend to make you feel stupid, but a sly sideways grin makes you feel as though you have a sign across the back of your jeans:"Kick me—I'm lost, and I'm stupid, too!"

REFLECT:

• What are some of the "body language" signals that someone giving you directions would unintentionally use that might make you feel stupid.

☐ sideways glance

☐ smirk

☐ incredulous stare

☐ _____

☐ _____

What have you seen Christians do that probably makes seekers feel uncomfortable?

_____

_____

_____

_____

_____

• Circle the emotions that you experience when you are lost and feeling stupid. List others you think of.

inadequate

confident

peaceful

lonely

tightly wound

_____

_____

What emotions do you imagine seekers are feelings when they come to your church or group?

_____

_____

_____

_____

_____

_____

When lost people came to Jesus, He never made them feel stupid. Whether they were little children or adulterous women, He still gave them dignity. At every point, He allowed them to sense that He loved them and that He valued them as people. They were lost, but not stupid.

APPLY:

• As Jesus conversed with people, He gently met them at their point of need. Look up the following verses and identify the person with whom Jesus came in contact and the action(s) that Jesus used to help them not feel stupid. The first one is completed as an example.

• *Luke 19:2-10*—Zaccheus was told to come down from the tree. Jesus honored him by showing a willingness to eat with him (when very few people would eat with tax collectors).

• *Matthew 8:1-4* _____
_____
_____

• *Mark 10:46-52* _____
_____
_____

• *Luke 18:15-17* _____
_____
_____

• *John 8:1-11* _____
_____
_____

• *Luke 22:31-34* _____
_____
_____

Several of the people in these passages had no religious (Jewish) training. Jesus had limitless patience with people who were discovering what the kingdom of God was really about.

Many of the college students on your campus have not had much religious background. They may not know the language or symbols of faith that you take for granted. Think how weird baptism would look if you had no idea what was going on. Non-Christians may feel much more comfortable talking about the football team or their high school days than discussing a personal relationship with Christ. If they are upperclassmen, they might feel comfortable talking about their major. Use this bridge to ask about the technical aspects or the career prospects in their field. Acknowledge that you cannot understand the finer points of their major (if it differs from yours) without further discussion. Just as one cannot understand all there is to know about botany or accounting or engineering without clarification, one may not understand what it means to be a Christian with only one discussion.

Our inability to understand a different field of study doesn't make us stupid. Someone who has little familiarity with the language, concepts, and symbols of a faith in Jesus is lost and in unfamiliar territory, but he isn't stupid. Rather than assume that they know what you are talking about, consider these steps with lost students or professors on your campus:

• Discover and affirm areas in which people excel. Everyone is good at something.

• Admit that there are many areas that you know little about, fields of study in which you rely on experts for help. Affirm that you can learn something from just about everyone.

• Admit that information about Jesus, the Bible, and Christianity may seem confusing at first without careful and patient explanations.

• Affirm that they are capable, intelligent people who can understand the message of the Bible, evaluate the ideas, and make appropriate decisions.

Secular students are not impressed when we show off our biblical knowledge. Most of the time we do so out of our own insecurities. Jesus was sure of who He was and of the truth of the message that He shared. He didn't have to argue or belittle. He shared of the kingdom of God with compassion and understanding. If your seeker friends see that you are sure of a relationship with Jesus, but that you don't have all of the answers, they may be able to identify with you. If they see that you know where you are headed, but are still learning and growing, they just might feel comfortable enough to join you in your journey.

LOSTOLOGY LAB

• If you were graded on your attempts to make non-Christians feel like they are valuable persons, what would your report card look like? Give yourself a letter grade in each of the following categories and note what you need to do to improve.

☐ openness   _____

☐ approachability   _____

☐ helpfulness   _____

☐ patience   _____

☐ sensitivity   _____

☐ communication skills _____

☐ friendliness   _____

☐ acceptance   _____

• In your conversations with lost people who are beginning to ask for directions, what phrases do they use to let you know that they are concerned about appearing foolish?

_____

_____

_____

• What can Christian students in your church or ministry group do to help spiritual seekers feel more at ease and comfortable in your meetings?

_____

_____

_____

_____

_____

_____

LOSTOLOGY LAW #9: IT'S TOUGH TO TRUST A STRANGER

Have you ever been seriously lost—not just frustrated-and-mad-at-yourself lost, but *terror-in-your-heart* lost? Lost-to-the-point-of-desperation lost? No-end-in-sight lost? Terrified-of-the-next-step lost? Imagine what it might be like by blending two different possibilities into one scenario.

In Panama City, Florida, there is a giant maze. It is a wonderful amusement if you know what you are doing. The maze is built of fencing about eight feet high with many twists and turns and dead ends. The object, of course, is to find your way out. You pay your money and punch a time card to start. You then punch your card at various checkpoints (to make sure that you aren't climbing over or under the fences!) and again when you emerge at the finish like a triumphant mouse who found the cheese. Spectators can see the action from observation decks built high above the maze. You can actually watch people running into dead ends, wrong turns, and each other.

Now imagine that you are seven years old. What if the maze wasn't a game, but a place where you were sent? You wouldn't have the confidence to think that you could get out. You might not think to climb the fences until you found the outside wall. An unthinkable possibility might cross your seven-year-old mind—*I could spend the rest of my life in here.* Suddenly a man appears offering to show you the way out. You remember that your father taught you not to talk to strangers, but you are desperate.

REFLECT:
• Play a quick game. For each letter listed, think of an emotion that the seven year old might feel.

46

H _____

E _____

L _____

P _____

L _____

E _____

S _____

S _____

• Summarize the child's dilemma with the word that is spelled with the first letter of each emotion.

_____

Keep that emotion in mind as you think about lost people. The same conflicting emotions occur sometimes in persons who know that they need help but are reluctant to be identified as needy. They want help, but they don't want to rely on a stranger.

APPLY:
• What causes you to trust a stranger when you are lost?

_____
_____
_____

• Consider a desperate woman in Scripture. Read Mark 5:21-34. List emotions felt by the woman who was healed. (Remember that Jesus was a stranger to her.) Check any that might be the same as those of the lost child.

_____   _____

_____   _____

_____   _____

_____   _____

_____   _____

• It is tough to trust a stranger. Most of us had stranger-danger training before kindergarten. How can you tell a good stranger from a bad stranger?

_____

_____

_____

• If you are lost and need directions, what type of stranger do you talk to?

☐ strangers in convenience stores   ☐ strangers in gas stations

☐ strangers in fast food restaurants   ☐ strangers on the streets

☐ men strangers   ☐ women strangers

☐ younger strangers   ☐ older strangers

☐ strangers just standing around   ☐ busy strangers

We go through the stranger selection process without even knowing it. The amazingly simple answer is that all of us would rather get directions from someone we know and trust than from a stranger, any stranger. I know people who will pick up their car phone, call long distance to a person who knows a little about the city in which they are lost, and ask them for directions. It would be so much simpler to stop and ask a local, but that's intimidating and frightening.

Two things are important here. First, as lostologists, we can understand the feelings of students who are spiritually searching and need to ask directions. Second, we can remind ourselves that we would only trust a stranger if there were no other options.

Campus lostologists understand that when seekers recognize their need for spiritual directions, they don't know who to talk to. If they are far away from home, the emotions only intensify. So what do they do?

They might venture out alone to find a church. They could show up at the office of the campus chaplain if there is such a person. They might begin to sample campus organizations listed in the Spiritual Opportunities section of the school catalog. These steps require a great deal of initiative and willingness to take risks—more initiative and risk than many students will take.

Students who are looking for spiritual direction (though they would never call it that) turn to people they know. They inventory their friends to identify someone who is "into religion." Perhaps they would inquire about the sorority Bible study, or innocently ask about Baptist Student Union. In the past, they may have been in apathy mode with regard to matters of religion, but the pressures of being away from home or just being adults have intensified. They need a friend who can help them find answers.

REFLECT:
• In John 4, Jesus had a conversation with a woman at a well. To her, Jesus was a stranger. How did He lead into a conversation with the woman?

_____

_____

• How did He show compassion for her without making her feel stupid?

_____

_____

_____

• At what point did she trust the stranger?

_____

_____

_____

• Who else in the story came to check Jesus out? How many of them had to rely only on the word of a stranger?

_____

_____

The woman built bridges for others to cross. Lost students usually come to a relationship with Jesus by crossing over similar bridges—bridges of friendship and safety. I casually mentioned to my students that they should be concerned about bringing their friends to our group meetings. Katherine took me seriously. Two years later, three girls indicated that they were Christians because Katherine brought them to church where they heard about Jesus. Katherine built a bridge. Her friends crossed it.

LOSTOLOGY LAB

• List some places on campus where you can meet non-Christians. Now identify them as good or not-so-good places to have a spiritual conversation with someone.

Places	Good	Not-so-good
_____	_____	_____
_____	_____	_____
_____	_____	_____
_____	_____	_____

• How can you be a bridge to Jesus that your friends can cross?

_____

_____

_____

_____

• What are some ways that Christians can work together and build relationships with non-Christians?

_____

_____

_____

_____

LOSTOLOGY LAW #10: PEOPLE ASK FOR DIRECTIONS WITHOUT REVEALING THEIR TRUE EMOTIONS

You are sitting in the lobby of your dorm, waiting for a ride to college Bible study at church. Your Bible is open in your lap and you are looking over the parable that was studied last week. An acquaintance walks through the lobby and sees you. "What are you reading?" he asks. How do you respond?

There are several options. You can slam your Bible shut and say, "Oh, nothing. How does the basketball team look this year?" Or you can say, "I am doing my reading for religion class." Or as a newly certified lostologist, you can recognize that someone is pulled over asking for directions.

Think about when you are physically lost and have to resort to the absolute last option—asking for directions. All the streets and buildings look identical. You begin thinking of all of the bad things that happen to people who are lost. If you have postponed the inevitable until the last possible moment, you are probably late as well. Late for a class, late for a date, late for an appointment, late for a job interview. The law of lateness is that the anxiety level is directly proportional to the level of importance of the thing for which you are late.

So you ask for directions. You try to be as laid back as possible, as if you were asking about the best place in town to eat dessert.

REFLECT:
• When you ask for directions, which phrase most accurately describes your emotions:

☐ Excuse me, but I'm lost and stupid and wonder if you could help?

☐ Hey buddy, get over here now—I need help! Aaaaaaaaaaaaa! (accompanied by screams or sobs)

☐ CanyougetmeheadedntherightdirectioncauseI'mlostanddon't knowhereIamhelp!

• Which phrase most accurately represents what you will likely say?

☐ Excuse me, but my directions seem to be off a little bit…

☐ I seem to have missed a turn…

☐ You are my last hope in life. Where am I and how do I get to…

☐ Where is the library?

Why the difference between what you feel and what you say?

_____

_____

Unless you are very different from most people, you tried to look as cool as possible. The question you ask masked the emotions you felt. Your potential direction giver may have mistakenly assumed that since you looked calm and your question was controlled, you were all right. But your question did not reveal your level of frustration or desperation.

Jesus always tuned in to the people He met. He listened to their questions and noticed what was *not* said, discerning the underlying issues. He had the ability to look beyond the words and see the questions that were being asked in the seekers' hearts.

In John 3, we meet Nicodemus. A leader among the Pharisees, he was reluctant to let his powerful friends know he was talking to Jesus. So he came at night alone. Nicodemus began the conversation with what he intended as a compliment: *He came to Jesus and said, "Rabbi, we know you are a teacher who has come from God. For no one could perform the miraculous signs you are doing if God were not with him"* (John 3:2).

But Jesus saw that this casual conversation was really a cry for direction. *In reply Jesus declared, "I tell you the truth, no one can see the kingdom of God unless he is born again"* (John 3:3).

APPLY:
• Jesus knew what people needed to hear even if they asked about something else. Read the following passages and write what people asked for and how Jesus responded

• *Matthew 9:11-12* _____

_____

_____

• *Matthew 12:1-6* _____

_____

_____

• *Matthew 18:1-3* _____

_____

_____

• *Matthew 18:21-22* _____

_____

_____

When we talk with spiritually lost people, Jesus helps us see beyond what is being asked, to identify the real issue. As lostologists, we need to trust Him for such discernment. Even if you don't think of yourself as a "super-Christian," if you are a believer, you have a neon sign that says,

Come here for help. If a student who is not usually in your loop asks, "Can I talk to you for a minute?" be ready. The first couple of sentences are probably warm up words to see how you will react. The real issue is yet to come. When someone sends a signal that he or she is ready to discuss lostness, it is a big deal. We can be easily diverted from the seriousness of the plea if we aren't tuned in to some of the common, but subtle, signals. Assume that if any of the following things happen, a seeker is signaling spiritual interest:

The Question Signal: Listen to any question that has to do with spiritual matters. Seekers do not ask questions about the Bible or where you go to church or prayer groups that meet in your room because they are suddenly curious. God is at work. Take their questions seriously. Many times, these questions happen late at night or in casual encounters between classes.

The Church Attendance Signal: When other students ask to go to church with you (or show up at your church), you should assume that they are trying to make sense of spiritual confusion. The same goes for a dorm Bible study or a meeting of your campus ministry organization.

The "What are you Reading?" Signal: If someone asks about your Bible or picks up a Christian book in your room or even asks about your church bulletin, assume that something is prompting the search.

The Christian Music Signal: You are cranking some serious Christian tunes on your stereo. If a student on your hall stops and says, "Cool song. Who is it?" assume that this is not coincidence. Assume it is an opportunity.

The Fellowship Signal: It's probably part of your routine to ask seeking students if they want to go with you to a concert, ministry meeting, college class cookout, or movie night at church. When someone accepts your invitation, he might be taking a test drive to see if the spiritual road is one he should be traveling. He will evaluate the Christians he meets to see if there is anything about their lives that may supply needed directions.

The Antagonistic Challenge Signal: Beware! This one takes you by surprise. Someone is really on your case about your beliefs. They want to debate and argue with questions like, *Why does God allow this to happen?* or *What makes you so sure that God exists?* In reality, he or she may be asking if your faith has answers to difficult questions. You can't argue anyone into Christianity, but if you are honest and open with experiences that you have had and can point to difficult situations that Jesus faced, you may find someone who is asking for directions.

LOSTOLOGY LAB

• Recall some of the students you have encountered who were spiritual seekers. Think about the ways they signaled to you that they were searching for spiritual answers. Now discuss the following questions in your small group:

• Have you ever missed a spiritual signal from a seeker? What was the signal? Why did you miss it?

_____

_____

_____

• Why do you think many Christian students fail to catch the significance of questions and other signals that lost students give them?

_____

_____

_____

• What can help us as individuals and groups to raise our antennae to better receive signals that are being sent by students around us in whose lives God is at work?

_____

_____

_____

• In addition to the signals listed, which ones would you add to the list?

_____

_____

_____

LOSTOLOGY LAW #11: DIRECTIONS ARE ALMOST ALWAYS CONFUSING

I have a friend who gives retroactive directions. When she tells someone how to get somewhere, she ends her directions with something like, _If you get to the gas station, you've gone too far._ Think about that for a minute. It's almost a confession of confusion: _I know that you probably won't find what you're looking for the first time, so here is the first signal that you are lost._

The problem with direction givers is that the directions are crystal clear...to them. Residents of Portland know the bridges in the city by their names. (Go past the Sellwood then stay on 43 and take the Markham.) People who live in Atlanta know the difference between the thousands of streets with some variation of the word _peachtree_ in their name. In New York City, residents know that a borough is a part of the city and not something that a rabbit lives in. In New Orleans, people know that the section of the city called the Westbank is due south of the Eastbank section.

Direction givers struggle to explain the routes they follow automatically. It is especially noticeable when seniors try to give on-campus directions to freshmen. *Business building? Sure. Just go past the old alumni house, up to the corner where that oak tree used to be, past the Kappa Sig house, maybe a hundred yards farther up and you're there. Can't miss it.*

REFLECT:
• Recall some times people have given you confusing directions. Did they do any of the following things? If so, how did they increase your confusion?
• Assumed that you knew more than you did.

_____

• Talked too fast.

_____

• Used approximations of reality, particularly concerning distance.

_____

• Underestimated the difficulty of getting to the destination.

_____

The newspapers in Georgia told the story of an Atlanta Braves pitcher who was late to a game because he got lost. He was from another country and English was not his native language. A well-meaning direction giver suggested he take I-285, the interstate that loops Atlanta, but forgot to tell him when to exit. He drove in 70-mile circles for several hours. Directions are always confusing!

APPLY:
• Jesus spoke in parables to help seekers understand the directions. In addition to the parables of Luke 15 that we have already mentioned, He told of workers in the vineyard (Matt. 20:1-16); a banquet (Matt. 22:1-14); a narrow door (Luke 13:22-30); a Pharisee and a tax collector (Luke 18:9-14). Look at each of these Scriptures. Take your time. Identify the listeners and determine the central message of the parable. Notice that Jesus makes it very clear that salvation is within their reach.
• *Matthew 20:1-16*
         listeners_____
         central message_____
         _____

• *Matthew 22:1-14*
         listeners_____
         central message_____
         _____

• *Luke 13:22-30*
listeners_____

central message_____

_____

• *Luke 18:9-14*
listeners_____

central message_____

_____

The Pharisees confused people. Jesus came as The Way, The Truth, and The Life. He was able to make directions into the kingdom of God so clear that anyone could follow them. Those who heard Him didn't always follow the directions immediately, but they had them to use when they were ready.

Christian students are in a position to reach seekers like no other group of Christians. However, relating to secular people will require adaptation. We need to look at our expectations, assumptions, and vocabulary. Here are a few tips:

• Don't assume that secular students know anything about the Bible or spiritual principles. Even if they have a basic foundation, don't risk confusion. Build from the ground up.

• Don't use Christianese as your primary language. Use words that are common outside the religious world to communicate. References to redemption, atonement, sanctification, walking the aisle, and other theological terms usually leave non-Christians behind. These subjects are OK (in small doses!)—just make sure you explain them clearly.

• Take it slow. Don't cover too much material too quickly. Allow time before you go on to additional information.

• Don't be concerned if questions that non-Christian students ask seem unrelated to the topic at hand. Their questions reveal their interests. Respond to what they ask. Listen. Move ahead when they are satisfied with what has been discussed.

LOSTOLOGY LAB

• List four words we use when we talk about our faith that are confusing to someone who is not a Christian. Try to come up with four alternatives.

Basic Christian terms   Alternatives

1. _____   1. _____

2. _____   2. _____

3. _____   3. _____

4. _____   4. _____

• With a partner verbally give directions to a familiar place in your hometown. Without writing anything down, ask your partner to repeat the directions back to you. Were your directions easy to follow? Why or why not?

_____

_____

_____

_____

LostoLogy Law #12: Unnecessary Details Make Directions More Confusing

One of the churches I served had a security alarm. It was not uncommon for me to come in on Saturday and forget that the alarm was on. As I came in the back door (not the magic door where the code could be punched in), I would hear the sirens, and I knew that I had 90 seconds to do some kind of cancellation thing or the police would be called automatically. I would frantically call our staff person in charge of the alarm.

In the midst of the blaring sirens and the onset of a stress-induced headache, I would not have wanted him to say, "We got a great deal on that. It works with motion sensors. There are little magnet dohickeys on the windows and doors and if someone comes in, it trips the field and then the police come. There is an automatic phone dialer that calls the precinct and the cops are usually there within seven and one half minutes. If you can get to the touch pad and initiate the cancellation sequence within a minute and a half, you can abort the police call and we won't have to pay the $50 fee."

All I could think was *"The cops are coming again. I'll have an arrest on my permanent record."* All I wanted to know was, HOW DO YOU TURN IT OFF? (Have you ever heard the saying, "I asked for the time and he told me how to build a watch"?)

When you're lost and desperate, you don't want unnecessarily detailed instructions. You just don't want to be lost anymore. You need directions that are right to the point and are simple enough to remember.

• Imagine your ideal direction-giver. What would that person do and say to help you understand and follow directions?

1. _____

2. _____

3. _____

• Do you ever quit listening to directions that are too complicated? At what point do they stop being helpful and start being confusing? What are you feeling as you tune out?

_____

_____

_____

Jesus was remarkably clear when He gave spiritual directions. The disciples were constantly in His face about different things. Often, He answered their questions directly. Sometimes He spoke in parables to clarify.

APPLY:

• Investigate the question and the direct answer for each of the following references. Identify and write a sentence about what made the response so clear:

• *Luke 11:1-4*
      question _____

      answer _____

      The response is clear because_____

_____

• *Matthew 17:14-21*
      question _____

      answer _____

      The response is clear because_____

_____

• *Mark 14:13-17*
      question _____

      answer _____

      The response is clear because_____

_____

• *Mark 4:30-34*
      question _____

      answer _____

      The response is clear because_____

_____

When Jesus spoke directly, He was understood. When He spoke in parables, He made sure that they understood. When Jesus interacted with people, He carefully measured the dosage of truth that He shared. He was and is Truth. He knew all truth. Yet, for those who were seeking spiritual answers, He measured out the truth in portions that matched the individual's capacity to receive.

Many of you have had training in some kind of evangelistic presentation. They prepare us to be ready to share a testimony or a gospel presentation in a clear and concise way. Yet many of them involve the memorization of steps or stages, or even gospel overviews. If you bombard a student who is beginning to ask for spiritual directions with the whole load of information at once, you run the risk of overwhelming him. When seekers are in the early stages of their search, it may be more helpful to share information bit by bit. Here are a few practical guidelines:

• Listen as much as you talk. Earn the right to speak by trying to understand the point of view of the hearer.

• Ask questions to make sure that you are being understood. Stop every few sentences to see if there are questions.

• Use your memorized presentation as a mental road map to keep you on track.

• Respond to specific questions with information that you have committed to memory, but wait to be asked. You know where you are headed. It's OK to take your time getting there.

• Avoid sharing your faith in such a way that it sounds like a sales pitch. After all, faith is about people, not a product. If you are living what you are saying, sharing your faith comes naturally.

One final idea—sometimes on our campus, visitors will get confused as to the location of a classroom, an office, or the coffee shop. The most welcome words that a direction giver can utter are *Come on, I'll take you there*. Verbal directions, no matter how simple and clear, can never replace a real-live guide. If you are aware of a student who is asking questions and is spiritually seeking, it may be helpful to invite her to hang out with you and allow her to see your faith working for you.

Author J. Mack Stiles tells the story of an incident when he was a teenager. He and his father routinely boated in a small runabout in a river near their home. During the spring, the water was swift, and one day he found himself in the middle of the river in a boat with a dead motor. He was headed for the waterfall that went over the dam. He panicked. Though he could see his Dad running along the bank screaming something, he became distressed and paddled furiously with a water ski. His father got there in the nick of time in a borrowed motorboat. Stiles noted that his father was hoarse. He had lost his voice screaming, *Throw out the anchor*. Though Stiles related that he felt silly having forgotten the anchor, he concluded that sometimes we need a rescue, not instructions.

When secular students have pulled over to ask directions, they need both rescue and clear instructions. Most of us want to share the gospel with secular students. We desire to give clear directions, to be a guide to help lost persons find their way into a relationship with Jesus. If we are sensitive to God's leadership and sensitive to lost people, God will help us share the truth in the proper doses.

LOSTOLOGY LAB

• Write down two sets of directions to get from your house, dorm, or apartment to a place that you pick. Don't tell the others in your group what place you are thinking about (for example, the graduate library or the tennis courts). In the first set of instructions, let your theme be "The simpler the better." The shortest distance between two places is a straight line. In the second, pick another place on campus. This time, make sure that you include every detail you can about the route that you recommend. Then trade instructions and see if you can guess the places from the directions given.

(1)_____
_____
_____
_____
_____
_____
_____

(2)_____
_____
_____
_____
_____
_____
_____

• Role play. In groups of three, each of you give a gospel presentation to one of the others while the third person observes. When each person has had a turn, discuss the following question: When you talk with non-Christians about Jesus, do you tend to say too much or too little? Why?

☐ too much   ☐ too little

_____
_____
_____

• What changes will you make in the future as you interact with secular students to make sure that the spiritual directions you give are helpful rather than confusing?

_____
_____
_____

Congratulations! You have passed Lostology 201. Now you are ready to move into Lostology 301 which will stretch you to shift into search mode.

THE COST OF BEING LOST

CHAPTER FOUR

From the idea of giving and taking directions, our focus shifts in this chapter. Our profile as searchers is examined, looking at our lives as spiritual searchers who can recognize when someone who is lost. You are spiritual searchers, members of a search party that was commissioned by Jesus when HE said, Go into all the world... Prepare to examine priorities, redirect energies, and challenge perspectives as you join in.

THE THIRD 6 LAWS OF LOSTOLOGY
(Lostology 301)

13. A SEARCH REVEALS YOUR VALUES

14. SEARCHES ARE ALWAYS COSTLY

15. LOVE PAYS WHATEVER A SEARCH COSTS

16. A SEARCH BECOMES YOUR CONSUMING PRIORITY

17. A SEARCH IS ALWAYS LOST-CENTERED, NOT SEARCHER-CENTERED

18. A SEARCH IS URGENT BECAUSE THE LOST ARE IN DANGER

arah didn't anticipate this part of her assignment when she agreed to accompany a study group of underclassmen to England. The schedule was challenging, but not grueling, a mix of lectures and field trips. After a tour of Stonehenge, the entire group stopped to do some shopping. The plan was to meet at the station in time to catch the train to London. Eventually everyone got back—all but one. Megan was nowhere to be found.

The students were a diverse group, but Sarah had enjoyed traveling with them. Each person brought a different perspective to the group studies and each saw the historic places on their tour with a unique set of eyes. Of all the girls in the group, Sarah found Megan the hardest to get to know. Megan was an only child, and she hadn't liked sharing the sometimes cramped quarters. She was brilliant academically, and she made sure that others kept that fact in mind. Like many intellectually-gifted individuals, Megan was sometimes accused of having little common sense.

Now the famous English fog had settled in and it was growing colder. The last train would leave in less than an hour. The group was tired and growing more resentful by the minute. Megan was always last, not because she was slow, but because she preferred to walk alone. They always waited for Megan, but she wasn't usually so late. Gradually, the resentment turned to fear. Where could she be? How could she get in touch with them if she were lost? They hoped Megan would learn her lesson, but they were also worried about her. Sarah hurriedly devised a plan and sent several students back to look for Megan. Others stayed at the station waiting for her return.

It was Sarah who found her. Megan had not been listening when instructions were given to meet at the train station in time for the last train. She had ignored the admonitions to stay together. She had been wandering around for several hours and her self-confidence had crumbled. By the time Sarah found her, she was 12 blocks from the train station, and Sarah decided to pay taxi fare out of her own pocket. As they got out of the cab at the train station, Megan was holding Sarah's arm, looking very much like a wet puppy, complete with sad eyes, dripping hair, and drooping head. The rest of the group was tired and ready to get back to the dorm, but they welcomed Megan warmly and sincerely celebrated her return.

As Sarah waited for the other searchers to return, she watched the students express their concern for Megan personally. She wondered if Megan knew how much these new friends cared for her. ■

REFLECT:

• What motivated Sarah to organize a search for Megan?

_____
_____
_____

• Would you have volunteered to go with Sarah?

     yes _____   no _____   Why or why not?

_____
_____
_____

APPLY:

• Pretend that you are Sarah. Write out an action plan for your search.

    1. _____

    2. _____

    3. _____

    4. _____

    5. _____

• What would you have said to the searchers?

_____
_____
_____
_____

LOSTOLOGY LAW #13:
A SEARCH REVEALS YOUR VALUES

When I was in high school, I was a custodian at a public school. Part of my job was to clean underneath the bleachers in the gymnasium. After a basketball game, it was particularly nasty under there, but it was always amazing to me to find things that people had dropped. Of course there were peanut shells, popcorn boxes, candy wrappers—the usual trash that spectators intended to pitch underneath the stands. I also found things that I don't think they meant to throw away. Wallets. Driver's licenses. Car keys. Wedding rings. I tried to imagine the scene the night before when they realized that their valued items were missing. Did they try to go under the stands? Perhaps they were on hands and knees, picking through the nasty garbage, hoping to glance down in the semi-darkness to see a glimmer of their prized possession.

The scene is a familiar one. When we lose something, we look for it. The duration and intensity of the search are usually related to the value of the item or the consequences associated with not finding it. A search always reveals our values.

REFLECT:
• Recall two things you've lost—one you searched for and one you didn't.
  I lost and searched for _____

  I lost but didn't search for _____

• Thinking about the item that you searched for, consider these questions:
  Why did you search?_____
  _____

  How long did you search?_____

  If your search was successful, how did you feel?_____
  _____

  If your search was unsuccessful, how did you feel?_____
  _____

• Now think about the item you didn't look for. Consider these questions:
  Why didn't you search?_____
  _____

  How did you feel about losing the item?_____
  _____

  What did you do to compensate for the loss?_____
  _____

We don't stop to think about the search for lost items. We either search or we do not search. We make a mental checklist (that we don't even realize we have) to determine how hard we will look. There are some truths about searches:
  • Actions, not words reveal our values.
  • Losing items of minimal value is an inconvenience. Losing items of great value is a tragedy.
  • Not all valuables are replaceable.
  • The value of some items is determined by the consequences of not finding them.

If we switch our focus from lost things to lost people, the perspective changes. If a search always reveals our values, what does a lack of evangelism reveal? As lostologists, we know the answer: no search, no value.

Jesus had a clear understanding of why He was on this planet. Even though many people tried to give Him many other job descriptions, His purpose was clear. You can find it in Luke 19:10. Write out His Mission Statement here: Jesus came to

_____

_____

_____

His mission statement was based on the value system of His Father. Look up the following verses to get a glimpse of what God has always been up to. List the key idea in each passage.

- Genesis 3:8-9_____
- Ezekiel 34:16_____
- Matthew 10:6-7_____
- John 3:16_____
- 1 John 4:9 _____

Jesus' mission on earth centered on searching for lost people. He personally searched for lost persons. He interacted with lost people, taught lost people, ate with lost people, and answered questions for lost people. He also enlisted and trained a search and rescue team. His final words to the disciples were to launch a worldwide effort to find the lost. Jesus taught and empowered His disciples for more than three years. They weren't too quick at first, but eventually they caught on to the multiplication principle. We know of the gospel because the disciples taught others how to search for lost people.

If a search reveals our values, Jesus' values were crystal clear. People mattered to Him because people mattered to God. He loved us. He died for us. He built the bridge for lost persons to travel on their way home to God. The apostle Paul expressed this thought when he wrote *"What, then, shall we say in response to this? If God is for us, who can be against us? He who did not spare his own Son, but gave him up for us all— how will he not also, along with him, graciously give us all things? "*(Rom. 8:31-32)

APPLY:

In spite of God's love for people, some of us still struggle with evangelism. Match the excuses that we have often heard (or used)...

_____ Evangelism is not my   A. training

_____ I just don't have the   B. non-Christians

_____ I don't know any   C. time

_____ I need more   D. gift

These and other excuses seem awfully weak in light of God's value system. If God loved us enough to launch the ultimate spiritual search for us, what should we do with the lost people around us?

LOSTOLOGY LAB

• Describe the search (or lack of a search) for the last item that you lost. Identify what determined the intensity and length of the search.

• Ask each person to identify the most expensive thing that he or she has ever lost. Tabulate the monetary value of all the items for the entire group.

$ _____ $ _____

$ _____ $ _____

$ _____ $ _____

$ _____ $ _____

TOTAL FOR GROUP $ _____

•How would you describe the difference between cost and value:

_____

_____

_____

• Circle the number you believe is the value you place on lost people. Draw an arrow pointing to the number you believe represents God's value of lost people.

no value							value beyond measure		
1	2	3	4	5	6	7	8	9	10

• How do you feel about the gap, if one exists?

_____

_____

_____

• Do you want God to change your values? If He did, explain to the group what would change about your actions on campus.

LOSTOLOGY LAW #14:
SEARCHES ARE ALWAYS COSTLY

On June 2, 1994, Air Force Captain Scott O'Grady was shot down over Bosnia. The F-16 he was flying was cut in two by a SAM (Surface to Air Missile) shot from a truck driven by a Serbian soldier. O'Grady was able to eject, but the bolts that explode when the canopy of the cockpit blows off burned his face. He parachuted to the ground and hid immediately. For the first five hours of his ordeal, he lay face down in the grass, concealed in the underbrush with Serb patrols all around him. The soldiers would randomly fire rounds into the brush, hoping that they might hit the downed pilot. For the next six days, O'Grady lived off bugs and rainwater. He ate ants and grass and collected dew and rain in a sponge in his survival kit. He only moved at night, and he was in danger of hypothermia.

After almost a week, he took the chance that his radio signal would be heard by friend, not foe. The batteries in his portable transmitter were growing weak. One of the pilots in his own squadron heard his broadcast and an amazing rescue unfolded. Captain O'Grady was rescued by a team of 41 Marines dispatched from the U.S.S. Kearsarge, an aircraft carrier in the area. The cost of weapons and machinery used to bring him home totaled more than $6 billion. In addition to the men who risked their lives to bring O'Grady home, the arsenal of machinery included:

- 40 aircraft and helicopters
- two CH-53 Sea Stallion helicopters
- two AH-1W Sea Cobra gunships
- four A-8B Sea Harriers
- F/A 18 fighter bombers (from USS Theodore Roosevelt)
- F-16s (from Aviano Air Force Base)
- F-15Es to fly cover and attack threatening ground forces
- AWACs spy airplanes circling high overhead
- Satellites positioned for the operation

Needless to say, they were serious about bringing one pilot home.

REFLECT:

• You are a Marine, painting your face black so as not to be seen in the predawn hours of the rescue. Write a diary entry to describe your feelings right before your Super Stallion attack helicopter departs the Kearsarge. Dear Diary:

_____

_____

_____

_____

_____

_____

_____

_____

_____

_____

• How do you feel about the amount of resources invested to bring one pilot home safely?

_____

_____

_____

Whenever we read of a lost child or missing family member, we shiver a bit as we personalize the tragedy unfolding for another family. We know that if it were us, we would do whatever was required to bring home our loved one. Money would not be an issue. Time would not be an issue. Our only focus would be on the discovery and return of our family member. Even if we have never been through such a situation, we can understand that a search is costly. It would be expected that large amounts of time and resources would be given without hesitation.

Only in spiritual search and rescue do we alter these expectations. We want evangelism that does not demand time and church outreach that does not cost money. We somehow manage to take the faces off lost students that we know and minimize the cost of the search. Turn to Philippians 2:5-8. Notice the attitude that Paul says should be ours (v. 5). Look at the description of how Jesus gave up each and every privilege that were rightfully His. Notice the extent of His obedience (v. 8). The cross is the price tag for His search and rescue mission.

How odd that in light of eternal consequences, we change our value system. The Bible proclaims the incredible price God was willing to pay for a lost world, and we must be willing to have the same attitude even if we don't pay the same price. He paid the ultimate price for us. On the cross, God proved that a search is always costly. To think otherwise is to ignore the reason that Jesus died.

APPLY:

• If you were to see evangelism as a search and rescue mission, what would change about your

calendar? _____

checkbook? _____

conversations? _____

• What can you eliminate in order to free up resources for spiritual searches?

_____

_____

• As you contemplate what you know about the price Jesus paid as revealed in Scripture, take a moment to thank God for His amazing sacrifice.

Evangelism requires sacrifice. It was expensive to find us when we were lost. Others paid that bill. Now it is our turn. For many of you, your time in college will allow you to be around more secular people in one day than you will see in a year after you graduate. The sacrifice that you would make for those students must ultimately be measured against the standard of the cross.

LOSTOLOGY LAB

• Share with the group about some of the key people God used to "rescue" you when you were spiritually lost. How did they sacrifice?

• Role-play with someone in your group. One of you is attempting to launch a search for a missing person, but constantly complains about how much the search is costing in terms of time and resources. The other person can respond. Don't forget to switch roles!

• List a few ways that we as Christians expect evangelism to be convenient and cheap. What practical ways can we as a group of students change those expectations?

_____

_____

_____

_____

_____

LOSTOLOGY LAW #15: LOVE PAYS WHATEVER A SEARCH COSTS

As a youth minister I became adept in a never-to-be Olympic sport which is pretty much the exclusive domain of youth ministers and desperate parents. The sport is dumpster diving.

Our group was in New Orleans leading Backyard Bible Clubs and cleaning up several mission centers. After an exhausting day, we returned to the church where we were sleeping for our evening meeting. Janna, one of our junior high girls, came to me in tears. "I (sniff, sniff) can't (wail, wail) find (sob, sob) my (whimper, whimper)… retainer." After lunch, she forgot about her retainer, threw the sack in the trash behind the mission center and picked up a paint brush. Now she wanted me to find her retainer.

"Janna," I reasoned. "I'm sure the trash is gone by now."

"My Dad will kill me," she sobbed. "This is the second retainer I've lost this month. Puleeeze help me!"

I was overwhelmed with compassion and I really cared about Janna and her friends, so I agreed to see what I could do. Forty-five minutes later, our bus driver was watching my back, my wife was holding my feet, and I was pawing through the trash dumpster behind the mission with a flashlight. Finally I located the plastic bag that contained all of our lunch leavings. I spread out its contents on the parking lot and went through each wadded up bag until I found the prodigal retainer. It was an emotional moment—I was a champion dumpster diver.

68

REFLECT:

• Describe something strange you've done because you loved someone?

_____

_____

_____

• Would you have gone to look for Janna's retainer? If not (and I don't blame you), would you have gone to look for a lost child?

      ☐ yes   ☐ no

As we indicated in the last chapter, the whole priority changes when we move from things to people. Diving in a dumpster for a retainer is nothing compared to what we would do to recover a child who had wandered off. But it is possible to become numb even to people if we are not careful.

REFLECT:

• How do you respond to the tragic news stories and pictures of children killed or hurt, or teenagers who are homeless or abused, or college students who are assaulted or date-raped?

_____

_____

_____

• How do you respond if you know those involved personally?

_____

_____

_____

It is too easy to dismiss the stories as unfortunate and go on with our lives. If we know the people personally, we stop what we are doing and turn our full attention to the situation. It becomes a matter of the heart. When it comes to lost people, we simply cannot view the losses objectively like an accountant studying a balance sheet. We must use heart accounting that considers every person worthy of a search and rescue—even a costly one.

APPLY:

• How do you respond to the stories and pictures of secular people in foreign countries who have not heard the gospel, or runaway teenagers with no thought of Jesus, or college students who are living life far from God?

_____

_____

_____

• How do you respond if you know those involved personally?

_____

_____

_____

Look again at Luke 15. Let's focus again on Jesus story about the shepherd who had 100 sheep. One evening, upon counting his flock, he discovered that he had 99 sheep in the fold and one sheep missing in the field. As a good shepherd, he left the 99 who were found to search for the one that was lost. A cost accountant would say that such a move was ridiculous. One missing sheep would be an acceptable loss. A heart accountant would work from a balance sheet that views the bottom line from the bottom up. No matter how many sheep were in the fold, he could not rest as long as one was missing. One missing sheep was an unacceptable loss in his heart. Jesus was and is a heart accountant.

REFLECT

• Read 2 Peter 3:9 and write down the first principle of heart accounting.

_____

_____

_____

• Now write the second principle of heart accounting found in John 3:16.

_____

_____

_____

Heart accounting is extravagant. It doesn't make sense to cost accountants. Consider the cost of college ministry. Activities for students who don't have any money to put back into the offering plate? Ministry that will never pay for itself? Come on, they almost never join our church; the cost ratio is staggering. As an objective evaluator, the cost accountant would say, put our efforts and resources into a group of people who will show a return on our investment. The cost isn't worth it.

If you talked to college students who have come to know Christ through ministries like the one you are in now, they would have a different answer. To them, it was worth it. Their evaluation would be based on heart accounting. Churches and other ministry groups have declared the college campus a worthy ministry field, regardless of the cost.

Making wise use of resources is always a struggle. Don't dismiss the use of resources by saying to yourself, _I don't have any money anyway._ That may very well be true, but you have time. You have abilities. You have contacts. You and your friends are at a critical time in your lives. A large percentage of persons who do not begin a relationship with Christ by the time they are young adults, never will.

On May 20, 1995, more than 105,000 Korean students signed the Seoul Student Declaration in which they pledged to dedicate themselves to bring about global evangelization in this generation. Sixty thousand of them pledged to spend one year of their lives in a foreign country to help start churches. College students can be involved in search and rescue. Priorities will always compete for your time and energy. Consider the following criteria to help you in determining how to use resources:

• Window of Opportunity—as college students, you have a unique opportunity to reach lost students that you may not have in the future.

• Immediate Accountability—determine how many of your resources are given to search and rescue of lost students compared to what you allocate to ministry and fellowship with believers.

• Spiritual Values—determine if your spiritual values concerning the lost are consistent with those Jesus demonstrated. Our actions reveal our values.

• Ultimate Accountability—we will use our resources somehow. No matter what we decide, we must be prepared to account to God for how we invested the resources He entrusted to us.

LOSTOLOGY LAB

• If you had been with the shepherd the night he left the 99 to look for the one lost sheep in the field, what would you have told him? Would you have affirmed his decision? Why or why not?

_____
_____
_____

• In your personal life, what system of accounting drives the decisions you make about the time and money you spend on search and rescue? Are you a cost accountant or a heart accountant?

_____
_____
_____

LOSTOLOGY LAW #16: A SEARCH BECOMES YOUR CONSUMING PRIORITY

My friends Dennis and Judy Rogers journeyed through the worst nightmare possible in December 1992, as they became involved in a search for their lost daughter. Twenty-year-old Jenny, a nursing student at Georgia Baptist Medical Center, was missing. Dennis was in Nashville for a meeting, and Judy was at home. At 4:30 a.m., Judy was awakened by a phone call from one of Jenny's friends. He had planned to meet Jenny after work the night before. "I can't find her and I'm scared," he said. Judy knew something was wrong. Jenny was too responsible just to disappear. The search began.

Judy and Jenny's friend went to her apartment—she wasn't there. They called the police and checked the hospitals. No sign of Jenny. Judy finally called Dennis in Nashville at 7:30 a.m. Dennis immediately left for home, abandoning his meeting. Jenny's friend alternated between searching and watching the news. At 9:00 a.m., he saw a news report about a body that needed to be identified. He immediately called the police. Finally, at 11:35 a.m., a police officer came to tell Judy that Jenny's body had been identified.

Dennis called every hour on his way home. At about 10:00 a.m., Dennis felt a chill from head to toe. He knew that his daughter was dead. Judy commented, "A few hours became months. I had such a feeling of panic. While we didn't know anything, I wanted to go outside and just begin to walk the streets looking for her."

Lostology Law #16 is seen easily in their story: a search becomes the consuming priority. Sleep is secondary. Annual meetings are missed without hesitation. It can be no other way. The search trumps everything else.

REFLECT:

• List the steps you would take to find a lost friend or family member.

1. _____
2. _____
3. _____
4. _____

• What do you think if you haven't found what you're looking for before #4?

_____
_____
_____

When people are the subject of search and rescue, the search becomes top priority. The Bible tells us that, as a child, Jesus got lost. Every year his parents went to Jerusalem for the Feast of the Passover. When Jesus was 12 years old, they went to the feast, according to custom. After the feast was over, while his parents were returning home, Jesus stayed in Jerusalem, but they were unaware of it. Thinking he was with other relatives, they traveled on for a day. When they did not find Him, they went back to Jerusalem to look for Him. After three days they found Him in the temple courts, sitting among the teachers, listening to them, and asking them questions.

Everyone who heard Him was amazed at His understanding and His answers. When His parents saw Him, they were astonished. His mother said to Him, *"Son, why have you treated us like this? Your father and I have been anxiously searching for you." "Why were you searching for me?" he asked. "Didn't you know I had to be in my Father's house?" But they did not understand what he was saying to them* (Luke 2:48-50).

• What did Mary and Joseph change in order to search for Jesus?

_____
_____
_____

Jesus' lifestyle communicated His priority—searching for the lost. Read

Mark 1:36-38, when the crowds tried to control His agenda: *Simon and his companions went to look for him, and when they found him, they exclaimed: "Everyone is looking for you!" Jesus replied, "Let us go somewhere else—to the nearby villages—so I can preach there also. That is why I have come."*

What did Jesus change in order to search for other lost people? He told the disciples that they needed to move on—there were other people in need of the gospel and that was his reason for coming (Mark 1:38).

Now, go back to the parables of Luke 15.

Then Jesus told them this parable: "Suppose one of you has a hundred sheep and loses one of them. Does he not leave the ninety-nine in the open country and go after the lost sheep until he finds it? And when he finds it, he joyfully puts it on his shoulders and goes home. Then he calls his friends and neighbors together and says, 'Rejoice with me; I have found my lost sheep.' I tell you that in the same way there will be more rejoicing in heaven over one sinner who repents than over ninety-nine righteous persons who do not need to repent. Or suppose a woman has ten silver coins and loses one. Does she not light a lamp, sweep the house and search carefully until she finds it? And when she finds it, she calls her friends and neighbors together and says, 'Rejoice with me; I have found my lost coin.' In the same way, I tell you, there is rejoicing in the presence of the angels of God over one sinner who repents" Luke 15:3-10.

Change your focus for a minute. Look at those verses again, but this time, imagine that you are the shepherd. It has been a long day and you are ready to turn in. There is a good basketball game on the tube and you are already in recliner mode. The final thing to do is to count. What changes when you can't go from 99 to 100?

Think about the woman with the lost coin. She was going about her day, cleaning, dusting, watching the soaps. Then she realized that one of her prized coins was missing. She forgot any plans that she might have had. A lost valuable changed her focus.

Now look at a fascinating passage of Scripture. We don't look in the Book of Acts for the words of Jesus often, but it is appropriate here. *So when they met together, they asked him, "Lord, are you at this time going to restore the kingdom to Israel?" He said to them: "It is not for you to know the times or dates the Father has set by his own authority. But you will receive power when the Holy Spirit comes on you; and you will be my witnesses in Jerusalem, and in all Judea and Samaria, and to the ends of the earth"* (Acts 1:6-8).

• What was the top priority in the minds of the disciples?

_____

_____

• What was the top priority in the mind of Jesus?

_____

_____

Some churches today see themselves as search and rescue churches. They exist for people who aren't there. Essential elements for spiritual growth like quiet time, Bible study, prayer, worship, ministry, and fellowship with Christian students all take chunks of time. Evangelism can be out of sight and out of mind. It's not that evangelism is unimportant. We simply pay attention to other things, both secular and spiritual, until there is no time left to share our faith. It may be helpful to evaluate and focus to move reaching the lost up the priority ladder just a bit.

• Who is the primary beneficiary of your ministry on campus?
_____
_____

• Who is the primary beneficiary of your college class at church?
_____
_____

• Keep a list of lost people you know and pray for them. Ask God to give you an opportunity to talk to them, and trust that He will be working on their hearts.

• Learn to use a gospel tract and keep one with you. Even if you don't feel that the time is right to talk to someone at length, you can offer the tract and look for an opportunity to follow up later.

Evangelism does not always come easy. Without making sure that it is high on our list, we may find ourselves going for weeks and months without ever talking to anyone about a relationship with Christ. As lostologists, we must commit ourselves to being available for search and rescue.

LOSTOLOGY LAB

• Recall a time when you lost something valuable enough to change your plans for a search. Explain what made the search your number one priority.

• Role-play this scene: You are in the student center. The perfect opportunity for search and rescue presents itself. A student with whom you have had some conversations in class is sitting by herself. You know that she is spiritually lost. What will you say when you approach her?

• How do you deal with competing priorities at college? Do a one-word round-robin with your group. Identify things that compete for your attention. When each person has named four things, discuss how to arrange your time so that the most important things receive the most time.

(1)_____
(2)_____
(3)_____
(4)_____

74

LOSTOLOGY LAW #17: A SEARCH IS ALWAYS LOST-CENTERED, NOT SEARCHER-CENTERED

Imagine that a little girl named Amanda has been lost. You've heard the appeal for volunteer searchers and have decided to help. When you arrive at the base camp for the search, you're shocked by what you see.

Along the edge of the woods, people have parked motor homes and travel trailers. Volunteers sit in lawn chairs around roaring fires between the campsites. On the grills, steaks are cooking. Music plays. Laughter fills the air. Those sitting around the fires occasionally look at maps. A few of the men tell stories of searches they have been part of in the past. You hear of the great flood of '65 or the tornado of '79. Occasionally, the search coordinator walks to the edge of the woods and calls out, "Amanda. Amanda. Come here if you can hear me." Then he returns to the group by the fire.

You are stunned. You cannot even believe that they call this a search. So you approach the search coordinator and ask, "What are you doing? A little girl is lost out there and you guys sit around in your Winnebagos and swap stories! Why aren't you looking for her?"

He seems confused. "Hold on a minute," he replies. "Some of these folks came a long way. We have to get ready. Now is the time to eat and relax. But we'll keep our eyes open. Who knows? We might just find her."

What's wrong with this picture? The rescue effort is searcher-centered. The focus is on the searchers, their comfort, and their convenience. In contrast, a true search is always lost-centered.

REFLECT:
• What would you have felt if you had volunteered and found this scene?

      ☐ How can this be happening?

      ☐ If this is the plan, I'm outta here.

      ☐ Someone should do something.

      ☐ Who's in charge of this mess?

      ☐ Seems like a good plan to me.

• Do you see any parallels with the way we do evangelistic searches, both as individuals and as churches or campus groups? What are they?

_____
_____
_____
_____

• What would have motivated you to volunteer to search for Amanda in the first place?

_____

_____

_____

• List the first five orders you would give the searchers if you were in charge of the search for Amanda.

1. _____

2. _____

3. _____

4. _____

5. _____

You probably indicated that you would get the information channels open. *What was Amanda wearing? What does she look like? When was she last seen? What kinds of things does she like to do? Does she have any friends who would be able to help us?* All of the questions lead to the same end: How can I think like Amanda is thinking? You would be Amanda-centered.

Jesus was lost-centered. He spent His whole adult life around lost people. Rather than hanging around the religious leaders or even His relatives, Jesus chose to live among the spiritually needy. Prostitutes and tax collectors approached Jesus when they needed help. All kinds of lost people sought Him out.

Jesus' lost-centered life bothered His critics. They accused Him of all sorts of things. If He were on your campus, Jesus would be seen with fraternity men, cheerleaders, nerds, foreign students, graduate assistants—any group that includes lost people. He probably wouldn't be hanging around your campus ministry group. Jesus simply indicated that since He was a spiritual doctor; it made more sense for Him to be around the sick. The disciples slowly caught on.

You can make some minor adjustments in your life on campus and begin to be more lost-centered. The easiest way is to take advantage of the natural settings for being around secular people. You sit by such students every day in at least one of your classes. Even if you go to a religious school, there are lost students in your classes. They are also in your clubs, on your intramural team, in student government. They are students, faculty, administration, university staff. They are cafeteria workers and math professors and resident assistants in dormitories.

In addition to meeting lost people in the everyday patterns of campus life, you can go out of your way to be lost-centered. Every Thursday, a group of students from a school in New Orleans go to the French Quarter to minister to homeless teenagers. Many of these teenagers are homeless by choice, drawn to the South because of the climate. It is tough ministry, but for the students who go to the Quarter, it is rewarding. Lost-centered ministry usually is. Many churches are taking a similar look at the way they do business. Rather than settling for a searcher-centered existence, these churches are becoming lost-centered. As they make this shift, they refuse to compromise the message of the gospel. They strive to go where lost people are.

APPLY:
• Here are some practical ways that we can keep the search lost-centered. Add your own suggestions to the list.
> • Meet the physical and emotional needs of the lost.
> • Go to the lost rather than expecting them to come to you.
> • Value non-Christians as people and seek to develop relationships with them. Never view them as your evangelism projects. No one wants to be a project.
> • Lovingly challenge your non-Christian friends to commit their lives to Christ. Give them time, but do not allow them to become comfortable in an in-between state.
> • Devote some campus ministry meeting time to learning about lost people.
> •
>
> •
>
> •
>
> •

Unless we take specific steps to remain lost-centered, we will begin the subtle shift illustrated in the story below. We must not allow this story to be a parable of college ministry in the 1990s. Frank Voight wrote this classic story "The Lifesaving Station" which offer a much-needed reality check.

"On a dangerous seacoast where shipwrecks often occur was a crude, little lifesaving station. The building was just a hut, and there was only one boat. The few devoted members kept a constant watch over the sea. With no thought for themselves, they went out, day or night, searching tirelessly for the lost. So many lives were saved by the wonderful little stations that it became famous.

"Some of those who were saved, and various others in the surrounding area, wanted to become associated with the station and gave of their time, money, and effort for the support of its work. New boats were bought, and new crews were trained. The little lifesaving station grew.

"Some of the members of the lifesaving station were unhappy because the building was crude and poorly equipped. They felt that a more comfortable place should be provided as the first refuge of those saved from the sea. So they replaced the emergency cots with beds and put better furniture in an enlarged building.

"Now the lifesaving station became a popular gathering place for its members, and they redecorated it beautifully and furnished it exquisitely because they used it as a club.

"Fewer members were now interested in going to sea on lifesaving missions so they hired crews to do this work. The lifesaving motif still prevailed in the club decoration, however, and a symbolic lifesaving boat dominated the room where initiation took place.

"About this time, a large ship was wrecked off the coast, and the hired crew brought in boat loads of cold, wet, and half-drowned people. They were dirty and sick; some had black skin, and some had yellow skin. The beautiful club was considerably messed up. So the property committee immediately had a shower house built outside the club where victims of shipwrecks could be cleaned up before coming inside.

"At the next meeting, a split took place in the club membership. Most of the members wanted to stop the lifesaving activities as being unpleasant and a hindrance to the normal life of the club. Some members insisted on lifesaving as their primary purpose and pointed out that they still were called a lifesaving station. They finally were voted down, however, and told that if they wanted to save the lives of various kinds of people who were shipwrecked in those waters, they could begin their own lifesaving station down the coast. They did.

"As the years went by, the new station experienced the same changes that had occurred in the old. It evolved into a club, and yet another lifesaving station was founded. History continued to repeat itself; and if you visit that coast today, you will find a number of exclusive clubs along that shore. Shipwrecks are still frequent in those waters. But most people drown."

LOSTOLOGY LAB

- Discuss "The Lifesaving Station." and address the following questions:
  - What forces cause Christians to become searcher-centered?
  - How are those same forces at work in your church or campus?
  - How can you resist becoming like the people in the Lifesaving Station?

- Circle the characteristics which describe a lost-centered lifestyle.
  comfort   sacrifice

  awareness of others   ease

  a sense of urgency   plenty of time

  willingness to work hard   personal commitment

- What is the real difference between being searcher-centered and being lost-centered?

_____

_____

_____

_____

_____

Timberline Lodge straddles a line between trees and bare rock near the summit of Mt. Hood. Climbers challenge the mountain regularly, trekking to the summit ridge and back to the warmth of the lodge.

Three adults and nine high school students planned to conquer Mt. Hood in May of 1986. The weather had been questionable, but a break in storm fronts suggested they could complete their climb as planned. Several hours into their trek, the weather changed. Storms attacked with vengeance. Strong winds whipped, and blowing snow disoriented the climbers. They struggled to regain their bearings so they could retreat to Timberline.

Some of the students began to suffer from hypothermia. In desperation, their leader made the decision to build a snow cave for those who couldn't continue the descent. Three members went for help. Nine stayed behind. Eventually, the three climbers reached the lodge. Search and rescue operations began immediately.

The storm's fury hindered the search efforts. Knowing what was at stake, emergency crews endured extreme conditions to continue their search, but it was three days before they found the tiny snow cave. By the time the searchers arrived, it was too late. Only one of the climbers inside the cave was alive.

REFLECT:

• Rank the factors from 1 to 5 (1 is most important) that make the difference between a happy ending and a tragic one:

_____ commitment of the searchers

_____ searchers' appreciation for the peril that faces the lost

_____ speed at which the search team mobilizes

_____ understanding of the situation by the lost students

_____ providential help

• When you consider the spiritually lost, do you feel the same compelling sense of urgency that the search party felt as they tried to find lost students?

_____

_____

_____

So far in our study of lostology, we have looked at lighter moments. But lostology has another side, an intense and painful one. One of the truths of lostology that we don't like to face is that the price is steep for those who remain lost. The searchers knew what would happen if the students on the mountain were not found. Time was precious. Fear of the consequences drove the search party to risk their own lives attempting to save others.

Urgency marked Jesus' life. Every decision reflected His ultimate priorities. More than anyone else before or since, He understood the stakes. Jesus knew the reality of eternity. In Luke 16:19-31, He told a parable about it. Turn there and study the passage to answer the following questions:

•What is the most terrifying thing about hell (vv. 23, 24, 27)?

_____

_____

•What is represented by the great chasm between heaven and hell (v. 26)?

_____

_____

•What is ironic about the last statement that the rich man made (v. 30)?

_____

_____

Jesus was also aware of the reality of the cross. Luke 9:51 describes Jesus as setting His face toward Jerusalem. It is implied that He didn't stop along the way, for Jerusalem (and crucifixion) was on His mind. He summed up His urgency and mission when he rebuked the disciples (for wanting to call down fire to consume the opposition) saying, *You do not know what kind of spirit you are of; for the Son of Man did not come to destroy men's lives, but to save them* (vv. 55-56, NASB).

APPLY:
• Make a list of possible reasons why many Christians lack urgency in their search for lost people. Some have wrong beliefs. Some are unaware of what the Bible says about heaven and hell. Based upon what you know about the Bible, make your own list. Here are three answers to get you started:
> • Some question whether non-Christians are really lost. Don't all roads lead to God?
> • Some wonder if the lost are really in ultimate danger. Won't God give them another chance even after they die?
> • Some believe that after death, a lost person simply ceases to exist.
> •
> •
> •

No matter how reasonable and appealing these views may be, they deny biblical reality. However, what we say we believe often separates from what we do about what we believe. Put on the spot, many silent Christians would affirm that Jesus is the only way to God and that those without

80

Christ will spend eternity in hell. But if we really believed that the lost were in danger, wouldn't we act with greater urgency?

LOSTOLOGY LAB

• Write a list of statements that you believe are true about Jesus, the cross, heaven, and hell. Begin each statement with the words, I believe that. . .

I believe that Jesus...

_____

_____

_____

_____

I believe that the cross...

_____

_____

_____

_____

I believe that heaven...

_____

_____

_____

_____

I believe that hell...

_____

_____

_____

_____

I believe that evangelism is important because...

_____

_____

_____

_____

• Share the top three things that stop you from sharing your faith. .

1. _____

2. _____

3. _____

• What level of urgency do you feel personally about reaching the lost?

not much							great urgency
1	2	3	4	5	6	7	8

You've finished Lostology 301. You're ready to move on to the final set of the laws of lostology, some practical helps for the searchers.

Secrets Of A Successful SEARCH

CHAPTER FIVE

This section focuses on practical suggestions for the searcher as he or she looks for lost valuables. How will we begin? What resources do we have? How can we juggle all we do and do search and rescue as well? Tough questions. But this is graduate school!

THE FINAL 6 LAWS OF LOSTOLOGY
(Lostology 401)

19. COORDINATE RESOURCES TO MAXIMIZE THE SEARCH
20. DISCOURAGEMENT THREATENS A SUCCESSFUL SEARCH
21. WAITING IS PART OF SEARCHING
22. SUCCESSFUL SEARCHES DON'T ALWAYS HAVE HAPPY ENDINGS
23. IF YOU'RE SEARCHING, THE LOST MAY FIND YOU
24. ALWAYS CELEBRATE WHEN THE LOST ARE FOUND

James had graduated and had an accounting job with a big firm waiting for him in the fall. He wanted to spend his final collegiate summer doing something for the Lord. He had applied to the mission board, hoping for an international assignment. When the letter came in February, James was elated. Kenya would be his summer home.

James was assigned to work in a small village not far from Nairobi. His job was to assist a team of volunteer English teachers. He also worked with a local pastor, led Bible clubs, and helped a musical group prepare a concert.

One day when James (along with his translator and guide) entered the village, the atmosphere was noticeably agitated. Instead of the usual friendly greeting, the people were preoccupied. The schoolhouse was empty; the small cinder block church was silent. Two small boys were missing. They had wandered out of the village early in the morning. The leaders were preparing for a search. James asked if he could join them and they agreed.

The men formed several parallel lines and began to spread out in widening arcs. Each line included a first aid person in case medical attention was needed. Each line had an older man who knew the jungle. Each line had a relative of both boys. Each line had a communications expert who through a series of whistles let the others know how their search was going.

Finally, the boys were found. Like most little boys, they really didn't even know that they were lost. They had played farther and farther away from the security of the village. When the boys realized that the men were looking for them, they decided not to be found right away. They played a sort of a game, running behind trees, but they were spotted by one of the search lines.

After a good scolding, they all returned to the village where the mothers welcomed their children into their arms with elation. The whole village changed; silence was replaced with laughter. The lost had been found.

Later that night, James wrote this entry in his journal:

"I was impressed with the similarities between what I witnessed today and search and rescue operations that I have read about in the United States. On the one hand, helicopters, cellular phones, and helmeted National Guardsmen were absent. On the other hand, organization, communication, and coordination were evident. The men and women of the village appointed a team, gave them whatever equipment was needed, and dispatched them rather smoothly. While searching, everyone seemed to know his job and trusted others to do their jobs. I suppose that some things, like hunting for lost children, are just instinctive, regardless of the culture."

REFLECT:
• What do you think the villagers were thinking and feeling?
_____
_____
_____

• How do you think the villagers knew what to do?
_____
_____
_____

• What about the rescue changed the atmosphere in the village?
_____
_____
_____

• If you were James, based on your education and experience, what would you have written in your journal about the events of the day?
_____
_____
_____

APPLY:
• You are assigned to organize a search and rescue for some children who were lost from the day camp of an inner city church. Make a list of equipment you think you would need for the search. Make another list of the people you would need.

Equipment

1. _____
2. _____
3. _____
4. _____
5. _____
6. _____
7. _____

Why would you want this equipment?

_____
_____
_____
_____
_____

Personnel

1. _____
2. _____
3. _____
4. _____
5. _____
6. _____
7. _____

Why would you want these people to help you?

_____
_____
_____
_____
_____

84

LOSTOLOGY LAW #19:
COORDINATE RESOURCES TO MAXIMIZE THE SEARCH

What is the first thing you think when you hear the word, resources? Unless you're different from most folks, you equate resources and money. College students often think, "I don't have any money, so what's the point?" Resources are more than money. When an intensive search is underway, money is secondary. Coordination of all available resources is primary.

It happens when someone gets lost. The word spreads. Phones and doorbells ring as the news travels throughout the circle of concerned relatives and friends. People gather. A collective rush of adrenaline energizes the group. Do something. Get moving. Find them. The search begins, rescuers spread out—often bumping into each other as they leave. Such searches are high on energy, low on coordination. As students of lostology, we acknowledge that spontaneous searches can be effective. Occasionally, they find lost people. More often, they produce weariness. Extensive searches need more than activity. They require coordination. Law #19 summarizes this truth: coordinate your resources to maximize your search.

REFLECT:

• What resources do you have that you could offer a search?

☐ time

☐ energy

☐ a sense of direction

☐ knowledge of the territory

☐ money

☐ outdoor equipment (compass, ropes, tent, etc.)

☐ outdoor skills (hiking, climbing, etc.)

other _____

• Why would your resources be important to the overall work of the search team?

_____
_____
_____
_____

Jesus spent His ministry on a search and rescue mission. He moved among lost people, helping them to find the kingdom of God. And He was very, very good at it. He was a compelling teacher, a convincing preacher, a gifted leader. Yet, early in His ministry, He began to bring other people into the picture. He called them disciples. As early as Mark 1, He challenged Simon and Andrew. "Come and I will make you fishers of men," He told them. From the beginning, He was about making fishermen. Not fishing Himself, but empowering others to fish. Though Jesus was gifted personally, He had a view of discipleship that went way beyond His earthly life. The multitudes of discordant and bewildered crowds were potentially ready to follow Him, but Jesus individually could not possibly give them the personal care they needed. His plan was to call men who would do it for Him, even past the boundaries of His own earthly life. So He invested the majority of His time gathering, training, and coordinating a long-term search and rescue force. He enlisted His group of unlikely leaders and spent time with them until their lives were marked with His values.

APPLY:
• Read Matthew 9:35–10:14 and fill in the outline below. Finish the sentences that are started and add others as well. Get comfortable—this may take you awhile.

Jesus' Training Plan for Coordinating the Search
I. Jesus saw and understood some things about people that motivated Him to do what He did (see Matt. 9:35-38).
　　A (v. 35) Jesus traveled all over the place, proclaiming

_____

　　B. (v. 36) He felt

_____

　　C. (v. 36) He compared the people to a

_____

　　D. (v. 37) He described the work in farming terms. He called it a

_____

　　E. (v. 38) He compared the disciples to

_____

II. Jesus instructed the disciples about gathering the harvest of lost people (see Matt. 10:1-14).
　　A. (10:1) He gave them

_____

　　B. (vv. 2-4) He called them by their

_____

C. (vv. 5-6) He told them to go first to

_____

D. (v. 7) He told them to keep the message simple, saying

_____

E. (v. 8) He emphasized the importance of actions to match words. Some of the actions He challenged them to do were

_____

F. (vv. 9-10) He downplayed the importance of material things. He said

_____

G. (vv .11-12) He told them to search for people to host them who were

_____

H. (vv. 13-14) He warned them that some would reject the gospel. When they were rejected, they were to

_____

APPLY:
• What is the significance of Jesus giving the disciples authority?

_____

_____

• Why did He tell them to go only to the Jews?

_____

_____

• Verse 11 is an example of coordinating resources for the search. Explain.

_____

_____

• Jesus had a sense of urgency. Give three examples from this passage:
   1._____

   2._____

   3._____

Through progressively challenging circumstances, Jesus pushed the disciples to their limits and beyond, stretching their faith and building their confidence in God. Instruction was on-the-job, not in the classroom. In Luke 10, Jesus coordinated the resources of even more believers, sending out 72 messengers with similar instructions. They returned with exciting accounts of what they experienced: *The seventy-two returned with joy and said, "Lord, even the demons submit to us in your name"* (Luke 10:17).

Jesus affirmed them and continued to train and prepare them. Through crisis and pain, through joy and celebration, He molded them and equipped them for their mission—His Great Commission.

He did not rely on their enthusiasm or on their willingness to be busy. He modeled and taught them how to coordinate their search effort for maximum results. Every Christian should be involved in reaching people for Christ. This does not mean that we all work in the same way or bring the same gifts to the search effort. It does mean that we contribute what we have to the effort. When cooperation occurs, everyone benefits. The lost receive the ultimate benefit—they get found! The searchers receive the satisfaction of seeing God at work—and joining Him in it.

LOSTOLOGY LAB

• With your group, debate what the results of the search might have been if, instead of giving detailed instructions, Jesus had said "OK, boys, there are lost folks out there. Go get em!"

• Here are some tips about coordinating the search. Discuss each one and develop an action plan for coordinating the search. Be specific about names of people and groups of people who could contribute at each point:

1. Build on the enthusiasm and contacts of new Christians in your group. Working together, new Christians can invite lost friends to the group and longtime Christians can help supply answers to spiritual questions.

2. Identify and build on the collective strengths of your group. Individuals are gifted, but the group has a collective giftedness as well. What does your ministry do well? How can you seize the day with that collective strength?

3. Different members of your ministry move in different circles on campus. Identify all of the types of people who could potentially be reached by the people in your ministry.

4. Plan group fellowship activities and invite others to join you. Some non-Christians are surprised to discover that Christian students are normal people who enjoy life.

• Recall a time when you lost an item and had to look for it alone. Now recall a time when you lost something but others helped you search for it. Discuss the differences between the two experiences.

On a spring Saturday in April, 1991, Patricia Lidrich and Katherine Spencer went hiking in the Columbia River Gorge in the Northeast. They became lost, but no one knew they were missing until Monday when they didn't come to work. A search began Monday night and continued through the day Tuesday. Rescue teams scoured trails in the heavily wooded area. On Tuesday evening, however, officials called off the search, prepared to turn it over to police as a missing persons investigation. Relatives of the two women were not ready to quit. Disappointed that the search was to be called off so soon, they planned their own search. Officials understood their feelings, but warned the family of the dangers of such an effort. Katherine's brother voiced the feelings of disappointment, saying, "I think a person deserves more than one day's search."

Inspired by the family's determination, volunteers and the 304th Aerospace Rescue and Recovery Squadron continued searching. On Thursday, while investigating an area that the ground search had already covered, a helicopter pilot spotted the two women waving a blanket. Though frightened, cold, and hungry (They were down to 30 raisins!), they were in high spirits and good condition. Everybody celebrated.

REFLECT:
• What decision would you have made if you had been responsible for the official search effort in light of the lack of success and the enormous expense of continuing the operation?

_____

_____

• If you were a volunteer who agreed to stay with the family, how long would you have continued to search if the women were not found so quickly?

☐ another full day

☐ half a day

☐ three or four hours

☐ two or three days

☐ weeks, if necessary

What factors would have influenced your decision to search or stop?

_____

_____

_____

_____

_____

We can understand why searchers get discouraged. When we search with no apparent success, it's easy to believe the following lies:

It's really no use.
You'll never find them.
You might as well quit.

Even though these are lies, they are persuasive. Discouragement is the feeling near the end of the semester when papers are due, deadlines loom, and you don't seem to be making any progress. Capture that feeling and apply it to a seemingly futile search. Understanding this emotional infection allows us to immunize ourselves against it. Lostologists must manage discouragement. Fortunately, we have a few good examples.

APPLY:
• For each of the Scripture passages listed below, identify:
    (1) the source of discouragement,
    (2) what the writer said to do (or what the person(s) did) about it, and
    (3) a way that you could fight discouragement in the same manner

2 Corinthians 4:16
(1) _____
(2) _____
(3) _____
_____
_____

Galatians 6:9
(1) _____
(2) _____
(3) _____
_____
_____

2 Timothy 3:12-15
(1) _____
(2) _____
(3) _____
_____
_____

When college students rise to the challenge of reaching out to secular young adults and winning them to Christ, you can count on the rush that comes with a successful search and rescue. But you can also count on the intense discouragement that comes when you don't seem to be succeeding. There are some practical steps to deal with it Consider a few of them to prepare yourself:

    • Check your expectations at the door. Recognize that it takes time to reach secular students. Many are rebelling against perceptions of someone telling them what to do. They will not accept new ideas quickly.

• Be yourself. Don't force yourself to share your faith according to a prescribed pattern or script. God will use your uniqueness if you remain available.

• Meet with other believers for encouragement and prayer. Do not try to do search and rescue work alone.

• Separate what you can do from what only God can do. You are called to search and share. Only God can convict and convert.

LOSTOLOGY LAB

• One of Jesus' primary strategies for helping the disciples past discouragement was to pull His men away from the crowds to spend personal time with Him. What are the implications for modern lostologists?

_____

_____

_____

• How can you share your faith in your own uniquely personal way without relying on a prescribed pattern or script?

_____

_____

_____

LOSTOLOGY LAW #21: WAITING IS PART OF SEARCHING

The fraternity house in which I lived in college had one of the last examples of a truly wonderful tradition in the Greek system—a house mother. Not just any house mother. Mom Reid was 91 years old when I moved into the house, and she had been on the job for 15 years. When she retired from her real job (when she was seventysomething) Mom decided that she wasn't ready to check out of life, so she did what any self respecting retiree would do. She moved into a frat house. Mom had seen more than 400 boys come through the university. She loved each of us like we were her sons. She did emergency mending. She fussed when we got too loud. She waited for us.

She didn't guard the door every night to make sure that we were in, but she kept up with important events in our lives. When someone got engaged or accepted to law school or took a big exam, she was waiting to celebrate or console. When a new batch of pledges came through the door, she insisted that each one make an appointment to visit with her and to sign her book. When Mom died at the tender age of 96, she had a multitude of fraternity men at her funeral to tell her goodbye. Mom waited on us to show us that she cared how our lives turned out.

REFLECT:

• Ponder the agony of waiting. Imagine that you are anticipating graduation (hear the Hallelujah Chorus?) and have had a promising job interview. The last thing the interviewer says is, "We'll get back to you in a couple of weeks." How do you feel? _____

_____

_____

• Now think of a time when you waited on another person because you cared about how his/her life was turning out. Imagine your emotions if you were waiting on

> a roommate who was late coming back to school because the weather was bad

> a friend in the dorm who was out on a blind date

> someone you had been out looking for but couldn't find

How do you feel? _____

_____

Law #21 points out an oddity that could be easily overlooked: waiting is part of searching! By waiting, we communicate much about our attitudes and emotions. Waiting shows that we are preoccupied with one who is not present. As a youth minister, I asked Sunday school classes to place an empty chair in their small group Bible study as a reminder of lost students who needed to be reached. Waiting is a powerful expression of concern for the people for whom search and rescue takes place.

Re-read Jesus' story in Luke 15 of the prodigal son. Jesus tells us more about the father than about the son who left home. But there are some unanswered questions. What did the father do while his son was missing? Did he search for him? Did he try to persuade him to come home? We don't know. Jesus did not tell us. We do know what the father was doing when his son appeared on the road heading home: he was waiting.

Why didn't the father go out to find his boy? The answer has incredible relevance for ministry to lost college students. The boy didn't want to be found until he had a need that could only be met by coming home. The father was waiting because he had accepted reality: there was nothing more he could do. He had to trust forces he could not control to bring his son home. He expressed his love by waiting.

As we seek to reach secular students for Christ, there are many steps we can take. We can work to build relationships. We can minister and pray and seek to meet needs. We can explain and answer questions. But with some people, we come to a point where we have done all that we can do. That is when the waiting begins.

APPLY:

• Describe a time when you pushed too hard in your attempt to lead a lost person to Christ.

_____

_____

_____

_____

_____

• What would you do differently if you had a second chance?

_____

_____

_____

If we continue to talk to those lost friends about their relationship with Christ, it can become counterproductive. Perhaps you've seen it happen. A zealous Christian badgers a reluctant student until he is turned off by the whole thing. In some cases, the repeated discussions and rejections can damage relationships with secular students. Coming to Christ is a big decision. It can be a long journey for some. These people need a special gift from us—our patience and love.

A Christian leader went to visit a tribe in Africa. The people had anticipated the visit and were prepared to welcome their honored guest. One of the children, a young boy, came to her and handed her a beautiful shell. The woman admired it, smiled at the boy, and said, "Thank you."

The interpreter explained that the shell was extremely rare and could only be found in an area several days walk from the village. The leader was stunned by the sacrifice the boy had made for her. She turned to the boy, and through the interpreter said, "You shouldn't have walked so far just to get me a gift."

The boy smiled and responded, "Long walk part of gift."

When we search, we communicate that we care. But waiting is also part of the gift. Waiting is beneficial for the searchers as well. Waiting helps to remind us that God is in control. It gives us time to pray. It allows our faith to grow through testing. Searching is part of love's gift.

LOSTOLOGY LAB

• Discuss times when you waited (or were waited on!):
   as an expression of love and concern

_____

_____

_____

   due to concern about safety

_____

_____

_____

• Brainstorm the signals that indicate that it is a good idea to go into wait mode as you witness to someone rather than to continue to actively talk about Jesus.

• How do you find the balance between waiting and moving ahead with a strong witness for Christ?

_____

_____

_____

LOSTOLOGY LAW #22: SUCCESSFUL SEARCHES DON'T ALWAYS HAVE HAPPY ENDINGS

A ranching family in a small community was moving their herd of cattle to the winter grazing area. The teenage son Joe was working with his father and the other cowboys. One afternoon, Joe headed back to camp alone on his horse. It was the last time anyone saw him.

Initial efforts to find Joe were unsuccessful. The family asked for volunteers to help them search the wooded hills and canyons of the area. For days, the local media reported on the volunteers' search, but Joe remained lost without a trace.

As days became weeks, the family's sense of urgency increased. Winter was coming. If Joe was alive, he must be found soon or he would not be found at all. The search continued as the weather worsened. One week became two. Volunteers slipped away, sensing they were no longer looking for a boy; they were looking for a body.

Still the family searched. The father said they could not stop until they knew what had happened to their son. When the snows made additional searching impossible, the family gave up, but said they would begin again in the spring. They did. Months later a report filtered out to all who remembered the original story that a body have been found. It was Joe.

REFLECT:
• If you were Joe's family, would you have continued to search for all those months?

_____

_____

_____

• From your perspective, was their search successful in any sense? If so, how?

_____

_____

It is instinctive for us to declare that a search has failed if the lost are not found. But don't overlook these facts that are true about every search effort:

- Family and friends care enough to join the search.
- Schedules are altered, sleep forsaken, sacrifices made.
- Through the media, other people share the family's concern for the lost loved one.
- Love keeps people searching in spite of discouragement and fear.

The components of the search are identical. The only difference is the outcome. With lost objects, success is clear-cut. You either find them or you don't. Find it and you're successful; fail to find it and you're unsuccessful.

Not so with people. Nothing can take away the love and passion with which the searchers approach their task. As lostologists, we understand that the search itself has significance. It is both a process and an accomplishment. The fact that you search is a monument of love and nothing can tear down that monument.

APPLY:

• Carefully read Luke's account of the crucifixion (Luke 23:33-56). At that point in Jesus' search for lost people, what did He have to show for three years of ministry? Was His search successful? Why or why not?

_____

_____

_____

• As Jesus hung on the cross, having been deserted by most of His followers, He continued to search (vv. 39-43). Was He successful? Why or why not?

_____

_____

_____

Jesus, the first lostologist, shattered simplistic evaluations of the success or failure of a search. The cross proclaimed that through Jesus, God searched for the lost. Love was offered, even if it was rejected or ignored. No one who is lost can doubt God's love or His willingness to launch a search and rescue mission. He spared nothing. Paul was stunned by this truth.

What, then, shall we say in response to this? If God is for us, who can be against us? He who did not spare his own Son, but gave him up for us all—how will he not also, along with him, graciously give us all things? Who will bring any charge against those whom God has chosen? It is God who justifies. Who is he that condemns? Christ Jesus, who died—more than that, who was raised to life—is at the right hand of God and is also interceding for us...No, in all these things we are more than conquerors through him who loved us" (Rom. 8:31-34; 37).

Traditionally, evangelism has focused on results. Your campus group participates in an event or plans an outreach effort. Decision cards show that students expressed a desire to accept Christ and we determine whether or not the event was successful. Don't settle for such a simplistic view. You will not always find the lost, even when your search is intense. You will attempt to share your faith and be rejected. Resist the temptation to return defeated and discouraged. The fact that you attempted to help lost students find God has value. We want the lost to be found, but ultimately each person is accountable for the way he responds to Christ.

As Christians, we are also accountable. When we stand before God, He will look at us and say, "Did you search for My lost ones?" "Yes, Lord," we will respond. We searched. We didn't find all we hoped to find. Still we searched. Then our heavenly Father will say, "Well done, My good and faithful searchers. Well done."

LOSTOLOGY LAB

• Have a debate. Assign one team to argue that searches are successful only when the lost are found. Assign the other team to argue that the search is valuable regardless of the outcome.

• Identify the evaluation process that your campus or church group uses to evaluate evangelistic efforts. List specific events and note how you measured their success. Would you change your evaluation in light of this study? If so, how?

_____

_____

_____

_____

_____

• Reflect as a group and share honestly concerning the following possibility: If you were standing before God right now and were asked about your personal (and group) efforts in sharing your faith, what would you say to God? How do you think God would respond?

_____

_____

_____

_____

LOSTOLOGY LAW #23:
IF YOU'RE SEARCHING, THE LOST MAY FIND YOU

The Friday evening news carried the story of three-year old Joseph Leffler who was lost in the woods outside Estacada, Oregon. A massive search was underway. Joseph had walked away from home on Friday, telling his mom he was going fishing, His mom assumed he was going to the backyard where he usually played with his favorite pretend fishing pole.

Joseph was not seen again for nearly 48 hours. Searchers combed the area Friday night, Saturday, and into Sunday. The searchers were beginning to fear the worst. How could a little boy survive alone in the woods? The dreaded ended appeared inevitable.

Just before noon on Sunday, little Joseph walked out of the woods and went straight to Judy Magill who was coordinating the search dogs. He stretched out his arms and she picked him up. Then she carried him to the command post where he was placed in a helicopter to be taken to the hospital. He was checked our and released.

The front page of Monday's *Oregonian* proclaimed the good news, LOST BOY FINDS SEARCHERS. A phot showed Joseph in his mother's arms. He looked bewildered but well. Joseph Leffler was safe.

REFLECT:

• What do you think the searchers were feeling after searching for Joseph for more than 40 hours with no results?

_____

_____

_____

_____

• What was the role of the search team in the story of Joseph Leffler?

_____

_____

_____

_____

• What if no one had been there when Joseph walked out of the woods?

_____

_____

_____

_____

This raises an interesting issue. Are all lost people trying to be found? I remember a time when my son was temporarily lost. He was at a birthday party in one of those indoor playground places. Children crawl into places that parents cannot go, and they can remain out of sight for long periods of time. The best a parent can do is to catch glimpses of the children as they dart by on the way to another maze or ball pit. My son decided not to be found. He worked his way to a vantage point high above the whole scene. As my wife searched for him, he watched. He didn't want to be found. I'm not sure that all spiritually lost people are ready to be found right away. Sometimes they watch as searchers try to find them, collecting information and processing their decision. Our role as searchers becomes one of availability. We have to be there when they walk out of the woods.

• What if secular people begin to search for spiritual answers and cannot find Christians to help them?

_____

_____

• What can you do when secular people do not want to be found? To what degree are we responsible as spiritual searchers to confront people with their lostness and convince them to get found?

_____

_____

"Jesus loves the little children. All the little children of the world." (Don't you feel like singing?) There was a special place in His heart and in His lap for the little ones. In Mark 10:13-16, Jesus talks about children. This is a model of simplicity for seekers and finders.

People were bringing little children to Jesus to have him touch them, but the disciples rebuked them. When Jesus saw this, he was indignant. He said to them, "Let the little children come to me, and do not hinder them, for the kingdom of God belongs to such as these. I tell you the truth, anyone who will not receive the kingdom of God like a little child will never enter it." And he took the children in his arms, put his hands on them and blessed them (Mark 10:13-16).

Children love to play games—chase, hide-and-seek, kick the can. Many of their games have to do with searching and being found. Parents brought their children to Jesus because they saw something that they wanted their children to have. The disciples didn't understand that in the game of hide-and-seek, Jesus was home base and He had just called, "Everybody in free!" The disciples were locked on the idea that you had to be searching to find someone. Jesus understood that the children had found Him. He took the opportunity to explain that the whole process of salvation was one of trusting like a child. Like Joseph Leffler, the children were running into the outstretched arms of their rescuer. And Jesus received them gladly.

Jesus was accessible to lost people. He positioned Himself among the people. He was available to children. He stopped to help blind men. He conversed with women at wells. He even had time for religious leaders with questions. As He went through life, He watched for lost people who were ready to be found and welcomed them with open arms.

REFLECT:

• As you reflect on the way you came to Christ, were you rescued by a search party of were you one who found the searchers?

_____

_____

_____

• How can you tell whether secular students want to be left alone or if they are playing spiritual hide-and-seek?

_____

_____

_____

Jesus challenged His followers to be available to be found. *All authority in heaven and on earth has been given to me. Therefore go and make disciples of all nations, baptizing them in the name of the Father and of the Son and of the Holy Spirit, and teaching them to obey everything I have commanded you. And surely I am with you always, to the very end of the age* (Matt. 28:18-20).

Scholars tell us that the word *go* is not an imperative or a command. It is better translated, *as you are going.* As they went where they went, they were to allow themselves to be found. The challenge He gave that first search and rescue team extends to us today.

APPLY:

• Plot a "people map" of your normal day. Think through all of your classes and daily routines, and write the names of every person who is within 10 feet of you on a regular basis. Who sits near you in class? Are the same people near you every day as you eat? What about clubs, organizations, your job, your dorm?

SETTING	PEOPLE

• Recall recent conversations that could have indicated that any of these people were ready to "get found."

_____

_____

_____

_____

• List some ways that you could be involved in the lives of secular students if you intentionally place yourself where you can be found. How can you be more available in your

CLASSES?	CLUBS?	CAMPUS?	OTHER:

• How do you see yourself fitting in to the evangelism strategy of your campus or church group? Circle the phrase below that most describes your gifts:

conversation starter   gospel presenter

patient "waiter"   prayer warrior

• If all four types are needed to form an effective evangelism team, who needs to be on your team?

_____

_____

• Discuss the following questions:
Do the non-Christians on your people map know that you are a Christian?

_____

How do they know?

_____

_____

If any of them wanted to talk with someone about their relationship with God, do you think they would talk to you? Why or why not?

_____

_____

LOSTOLOGY LAW #24:
ALWAYS CELEBRATE WHEN THE LOST ARE FOUND

Celebration is the spontaneous response when we find a lost valuable—a person or a thing. Celebration is instinctive. No one has to teach us. Nobody has to say, this is the appropriate time to show appreciation for someone's attendance. Jumping and shouting is acceptable when a lost student begins a relationship with Jesus. When lost people are found, we celebrate. Our response reveals our values. Lostologists acknowledge that the celebration is as important in the search as the coordination of resources or the verbal witness or the patient waiting.

Law #24 is clear: Always celebrate when the lost are found. In some groups or churches Christians react to the news that someone has become a Christian with polite affirmation rather than radical rejoicing. Jesus does not consider such lukewarm response acceptable.

REFLECT:

• Recall the last time you found something that you thought was lost. What was your reaction?

_____

_____

• What is the response in your church or ministry group to someone becoming a Christian?

_____

_____

• If you have personally led someone to a relationship with Christ, describe your emotions when he understood and accepted Him as Savior.

_____

_____

• Celebration was the common conclusion to all three of the classic stories of lost and found that Jesus told in Luke 15. What is the reaction...
　　When the shepherd finds the sheep? (Luke 15:5-6)

_____

_____

　　When the woman finds the coin? (Luke 15:9)

_____

_____

　　When the son comes home? (Luke 15:22-24)

_____

_____

　　When the lost are found, we have a party. The urgency is passed. The effort was successful. When we celebrate, we gain confidence and courage for future searches. We also join a larger celebration—the angels in heaven are throwing a full-blown, high-volume, reasonably out-of-control party (see Luke 15:10).

　　In Atlanta, a mission church met with our church for Sunday night service whenever they needed to baptize their new brothers and sisters in Christ. They were an inner-city congregation, a mix of black people, white people, and brown people, and they knew how to rejoice. At first, it seemed odd to see large groups of people in the congregation standing and clapping and cheering when friends or family members were baptized. But I got used to it. As a matter of fact, I really liked it. Our church family loosened up a bit and began a custom that I also enjoyed. When a new believer was baptized, everyone who had influenced them spiritually was asked to stand as they were baptized. Both clapping and standing seemed appropriate ways to celebrate a successful search.

• How do you celebrate the end of a successful semester?

_____

_____

• How does a corporation recognize their top salespersons?

_____

_____

• How do good grades and sales quotas compare with persons coming into the kingdom of God?

_____

_____

• Name the people that would have stood at your baptism. Take a moment to write them a thank-you note. They will enjoy remembering the celebration.

One group I know of has birthday parties each month for spiritual birthdays. As students accept Christ into their lives, they record the event on a birthday calendar. When their rebirth month rolls around, they have cake and ice cream with those who are a few years older in the faith, but who came to the Lord in the same month. The celebration indicates that they place value on decisions to become a Christian. That value is kept at the forefront month after month. An outsider could easily tell what the group considered important by observing what they celebrated. Even if you don't worship and fellowship with a group that actively demonstrates spiritual birthdays, you can do so personally.

APPLY:
• Add to the list below ways that you can be joyful over the lost being found. Include quiet means to celebrate as well as more robust ones.
   • Send a personal note—even a birthday card.
   • Send a note to those who influenced the new believers.
   • Have a birthday party for new Christians.
   •
   •
   •
   •
   •

There are a lot of good ways to celebrate so long as you remember to celebrate. When we respond to the news that someone has been rescued from hell with an indifferent, "that's nice," it's a sure sign that things are not good with our spiritual condition. Celebration can be spontaneous or it can be intentional. It can be between two friends or it can be among thousands of worshippers. But no matter how, no matter when, we must take time to celebrate.

LOSTOLOGY LAB

• Assign a small group of three or four to role-play a culture that doesn't understand celebration. You must teach them all they need to know about celebration: what, why, when, where, who, how. Fortunately they understand English, but they don't understand celebration.

• Share with the group about the last time that you celebrated. What was the occasion? What did you do to celebrate?

_____

_____

_____

• If you didn't have a celebration when you became a Christian, plan one now. What will you include in the celebration? Who will you invite?

_____

_____

_____

_____

_____

_____

Well, you've done it. You've made it through all 24 laws of lostology. In the final chapter, we will look at some practical ways that we can continue to use what we've learned. After all, you don't want to let your education go to waste, do you? Take some time now to celebrate with your "graduating class"...then read on as we conclude our study.

YOUR LIFE AS A LOSTOLOGIST

CHAPTER SIX

This final section focuses on the practical
skills and understanding that you have gained in this study
and need to continue to develop in your life as a
lostologist. This section helps to sharpen the tools needed
as you prepare for search and rescue missions.

Karen couldn't believe it. She was lost. She was reluctant to admit it, but it was true. Nothing looked familiar even though she thought had followed the directions exactly. She retraced her steps to the west side of the building. She thought this was the main entrance but it didn't look quite right. She checked the address. She looked for an office directory or a receptionist. In such a large building, there ought to be somewhere to turn for help.

Karen was ready for her first day at her first real job. She had worked through the placement office at the university and secured an entry level position with a large publishing firm. Her interviews had been on campus, so she had never visited the main office before. She had talked several times with her new supervisor, Rebecca, since the interview, and Rebecca had given Karen clear directions over the phone. She even sent a city map with places of interest marked so that Karen could begin to get her bearings in a new place. Karen had passed the mall, crossed the interstate, and located the office park without any trouble. But now, she couldn't find the office. Or maybe this wasn't the right building after all.

Karen wanted to make a good first impression. She'd allowed plenty of time so that she would be early on the first day. What would these people think of her now? Late. Lost. She knew they'd be wondering, "Who is this person we've hired?"

Karen entered the first office she could find and asked to use the phone. She called Rebecca, but got her standard voice mail message. She waited for a receptionist and explained her situation. She was transferred to Rebecca's assistant. Cathy apologized for the mix-up and asked Karen to wait by the elevators. Cathy would come and show Karen the way to their offices.

When the elevator doors opened, Cathy rushed to greet Karen. Relieved, Karen eagerly followed her. Cathy, also relieved, explained that Rebecca had forgotten that renovations would be underway by the time Karen arrived. She had alerted Cathy that Karen might have trouble since the receptionist had moved to another entrance. Rebecca had been called out of town and could not be there to welcome Karen.

They had really wanted to make a good impression on the first day with a new employee. Now what would Karen think about these people who had hired her? ∎

REFLECT:

• What do you think Karen was feeling on this first morning of a new job and the unexpected difficulties she encountered?

☐ excitement

☐ nervousness

☐ anxiety

☐ eagerness

☐ fear

☐ other _____

How did her emotions change as the morning progressed?

_____

_____

_____

_____

• What do you think Rebecca and Cathy were feeling when they discovered that their directions had been inadequate?

_____

_____

_____

This situation illustrates two benefits of being lost. First, you have a purpose—there is some place you are supposed to be and you aren't there. Second, someone cares that you aren't where you're supposed to be—you have a significant relationship with the one who cares that you're lost.

APPLY:

• Where was Karen supposed to be?_____

• Who cared that she wasn't where she was supposed to be?

_____

• If Karen was a lostologist, list at least three things could she have learned from this experience of being physically lost that could help her understand and help spiritually lost people.

1._____

2._____

3._____

4._____

5._____

Some of your friends may have said that life begins after graduation. Others have honestly confessed that the thing they fear the most about finishing college is that they have to get a job. Still others have said that when you finish college, your education really begins. All of these ideas contain some truth. It is a bit fearful to think that all of the work that you have done to pass tests or complete projects is irrelevant to an interviewer for a company. At that point, you will have to summon a new set of skills—those that will help you blend your knowledge with your ability to get the job done.

You may find it hard to believe that after successfully completing a degree you have to prove yourself by applying your education. The real final exam is in the real world. Your book knowledge is developed and refined by your postgraduation experiences. The same could be said of lostology. You now have the book knowledge. You have completed the sessions and activities in this workbook. Perhaps you have practiced along the way. But when you finish with your studies, it's time to get a job.

In working through this last chapter, think about the job that God has for every lostologist. Envision how to use the new tools that you have learned. Review each principle of lostology. Don't think of this as a final exam. Think of it as assistance from the placement office—practical ways to apply your new degree in the workplace. Remember that as a lostologist, you know the directions that lost people need.

APPLY:
• Write the definition of lostology.
Lostology is:

_____
_____
_____

• At an Alexandria, Virginia church there's a sign that church members read as they exit the parking lot: *You are now entering the mission field.* As a new graduate in lostology, if you posted a sign over your door, so that you saw it every day when you left, what would it say?

_____
_____
_____

• Review the list of the 24 laws of lostology on page 113 and answer the following questions:
   • Identify the three laws that challenge you the most. Why?
   Law # ____:

_____
_____

   Law # ____:

_____
_____
_____

Law # _____:

_____

_____

_____

• Which law is the most memorable? Why?
Law # _____:

_____

_____

_____

• Which law is most difficult for you? Why?
Law # _____:

_____

_____

_____

• Which law(s)causes you to change your behavior as a Christian?
Law # _____:

_____

_____

_____

• Based on all that you've learned in your study of lostology, write your personal Mission Statement. (Review chapter 4 for Jesus' Mission Statement in Luke 19:10.)

_____

_____

_____

As we live each day, it is up to us to recognize the lost so that we can help them find Jesus. Remember that some secular students are having fun being lost. Be patient. It is easy to be lost, and hopefully they will realize their need in time. They may not recognize their need, but God will use you to increase their interest in Him. Your job is to be ready.

Each time you are physically lost, even momentarily disoriented, capture the feelings and remember them. Begin to see each situation in new surroundings as an opportunity to gain understanding and empathy for spiritually lost people. Note ways that others help or refuse help when you're physically lost, and adapt or alter your own behavior toward spiritually lost people based on what you learn.

Also remember the two benefits of being lost and begin to look for ways to relate these benefits to spiritually lost people in language they understand: (1) There is a place you're supposed to be--in relationship with Christ as your Savior, (2) Someone cares that you aren't where you're supposed to be. Because of His great love for us, God declared us lost and launched a massive search and rescue effort on our behalf.

APPLY:

• Write a character profile of a lost person. Compare it to the answers you listed in Chapter 1. Has anything changed?

_____
_____
_____
_____
_____
_____

As college students, you have the opportunity to develop many different friendships in many different places. Your conversations about God are an overflow of all of the other conversations that you have. Friendships with lost students are the first steps toward evangelism. But those friendships are valid even if there is no interest in spiritual things. God is constantly at work. Every conversation has the potential of spiritual significance. Secular students are slow to trust strangers, so don't be a stranger—build friendships! Questions could have significance, so pay attention when a lost person asks you anything.

What are some questions that a secular student may ask which could be an invitation for you to talk about spiritual things?

1._____
_____?

2._____
_____?

3._____
_____?

Within those friendships, you can ask your lost friends to be honest with you. Ask them what they think about church or even about the times you have shared your faith with them. If you have a good relationship, ask them to give you tips on the best way to talk to people about God. Ask them to evaluate a selection of gospel tracts and tell you which one is easiest to understand. You may be surprised by how freely some people will share their insights with you—if you have first built a relationship and are willing to listen.

As lostologists in a lost world, we must be prepared to pay the price for the search. We must evaluate our resources, and decide what we will invest. Our most important resource is our own relationship with God. It's like the story of a little boy who was trying to get his kite out of a tree. After much effort with a variety of additional tools, he still could not reach the kite. His father, who had watched the entire drama, walked over and asked what was wrong. "I can't get my kite down," the boy said. "Have you tried everything you can think of?" asked the father. "Yes, Daddy. I tried everything." "Are you sure?" asked Dad. "I'm sure," answered the boy. "You haven't tried everything," said the father. "You haven't asked me to help."

As we commit to living in search mode, our personal spiritual discipline becomes increasingly important. Our prayer, quiet time, personal Bible study, and group accountability help strengthen our relationship with God so He can use us to seek the lost.. We have incredible resources, but we must never forget what is at stake.

In a discipleship group that I lead, one of the young men shared that during the past week, his wife's uncle had committed suicide. He stated it plainly and bluntly—so much that it took the rest of the group off guard, "And I know that he is in hell right now." Yes, the stakes are high. As we encounter lost people, we have to let the reality of hell create an appropriate sense of urgency in our hearts as we seek to share Christ with them. They are in danger of spending eternity without God. Your search is a race against time.

In addition to what you've learned in the 24 laws of lostology, there are some practical skills that will enhance your ability to give spiritually lost people directions to find Christ.

PERSONAL TESTIMONY:

Write out your own story as a lostologist so you will be ready when someone asks you for spiritual directions.

My Story

How I discovered that I was spiritually lost:

_____

_____

_____

_____

How I learned about the search and rescue mission that God launched to find me:

_____

_____

_____

_____

How I "got found":

_____

_____

_____

_____

How my life has changed since God rescued me and let me begin an eternal relationship with Him:

_____

_____

_____

_____

• Swap your written testimony with a partner and help each other cull unnecessary details which might confuse a non-Christian. Look for specific words or terms which non-Christians would not know, and suggest questions a non-Christian might ask as a result of each testimony. Revise your testimony as necessary and begin to practice telling your story and answering questions clearly.

USING SCRIPTURE AND TRACTS:

Key verses that you memorize can help you give clear directions to give to persons who stop and ask. Many people use the following verses from Romans, and many easy-to-use gospel tracts offer clear instructions on how to become a Christian. Ask your pastor or campus minister for samples of tracts and suggestions of other Scriptures you need to know in order to clearly and briefly share the plan of salvation.

Write out the verses below and begin working to memorize them:
• *Romans 3:23*

_____

_____

• *Romans 6:23*

_____

_____

• *Romans 5:8*

_____

_____

• *Romans 10:9-10*

_____

_____

RESPONDING TO DIRECTION-SEEKING STATEMENTS:

Always be ready to explain the next step to someone who is seeking direction. Here is a chance to practice. Write out your response to the following statements or questions:

I need to get some things straight first. What's the hurry?

_____

_____

_____

_____

Why should I believe in a God who lets people suffer?

_____

_____

_____

_____

The church is full of hypocrites. I'm as good as any of the people I know who go to church.

_____

_____

_____

_____

I just feel so empty. Is there really any meaning in life?

_____

_____

_____

_____

LIVING AS A LOSTOLOGIST:

The call to follow Christ is a call to live in search mode. We must go to a world lost and disoriented. Remember these things that will help you live as a lostologist:

• Non-Christians never intended to get lost spiritually. Never assume they chose to mess up their lives and therefore deserve what has happened to them. It is easy to get lost. Remembering this will make you more gracious as you deal with seekers.

• Watch for any indication that non-Christians sense they are lost, but don't try to force them to admit it. Awareness of their own situation is the turning point in their spiritual direction.

• Be a trustworthy friend. Don't flaunt your Bible knowledge or spiritual insights; you'll make seekers feel stupid just because they're lost. Listen to their questions. Go slow. Pay attention and be patient.

• Prepare yourself for *search mode*. Make time in your schedule to search for those who are lost, and be prepared to pay the cost in time, money, and commitment. Ask God to prepare your heart.

• Take the initiative to go into their world rather than waiting for seekers to come to you.

• Continue to develop your skills in reaching non-Christians. Work with other Christians to multiply your effectiveness.

• Don't give up. Look to Christian friends for encouragement and take time to renew yourself so that you don't get discouraged.

• Never stop seeking the lost. Sometimes you have to shift into the "waiting phase." Other times the seeker will find you.

• Thank God for the opportunity to live in *search mode*. Ask Him for strength, patience, discernment, a sense of urgency, and a love for all people.

• Celebrate whenever the lost are found. Involve others in the celebration as you welcome the lost home. Use this as an opportunity to introduce new believers to a family of faith.

THE 24 LAWS OF LOSTOLOGY

1. Being lost can be fun.
2. No one gets lost on purpose.
3. It is easy to get lost.
4. You can be lost and not know it.
5. You cannot force people to admit they are lost.
6. Admitting you are lost is the first step in the right direction.
7. When you are lost, you are out of control.
8. Just because you are lost does not mean you are stupid.
9. It is tough to trust a stranger.
10. People ask for directions without revealing their true emotions.
11. Directions are always confusing.
12. Unnecessary details make directions more confusing.
13. A search reveals your values.
14. Searches are always costly.
15. Love pays whatever a search costs.
16. A search becomes your consuming priority.
17. A search is always lost-centered, not searcher-centered.
18. A search is urgent because the lost are in danger.
19. Coordinate resources to maximize the search.
20. Discouragement threatens a successful search.
21. Waiting is part of searching.
22. Successful searches do not always have happy endings.
23. If you are searching, the lost may find you.
24. Always celebrate when the lost are found.

Well, that's it. You know the definition of lostology., you're ready to use what you have learned to understand and help spiritually lost people. You're ready to give them directions to God. Remember that this is only the beginning. As a lostologist, you will continue to learn more every time you lose your way. So the next step in your training is easy—GET LOST!

LEADER HELPS

This section is designed to help you facilitate a small group study of lostology.

Follow the suggested outline or adapt it as necessary for a quality learning

experience for your students.

Read this book carefully. Read each law and complete each activity for yourself. Become as familiar as you can with the content of each unit and begin looking for current examples from news accounts, television, and movies so that you can make the group sessions up-to-date and relevant for your students.

Read John Kramp's *Out of Their Faces and Into Their Shoes* to enhance your study and give greater understanding for you as a leader.

Advertise the study and date you plan to begin. Enlist students who are creative and artistic to help with advertising. Include currents news stories or headlines as appropriate to stimulate interest.

Emphasize the need for six weeks of participation from each student who decides to participate. Students should be aware of the individual work which is a part of this study. Enlist a group of 10-12 students for optimal group experience.

Order a copy of *Into Their Shoes* for each participant. Distribute books before the first group session, if possible. Encourage students to bring their books to each group session along with pencil, paper, and a Bible.

Secure a comfortable and quiet meeting room. Students will need space to write easily and talk freely among themselves.

Obtain other equipment as needed. You may prefer to lead group sessions using overhead cels of certain Scripture passages for reference or for enlarging particular activities. If so, prepare these ahead of time and be sure that the projector is working properly. You may want to have a chalkboard or flip chart available for listing answers in group discussion. Whatever teaching methods are most comfortable for you will be easy to adapt in the group sessions.

Begin praying for an openness and enthusiasm among the participants.

OVERVIEW OF THE TEXT

Into Their Shoes is organized in six chapters. The first and last chapters will be different because they do not include specific study of the laws of lostology. Chapter 1 is an introduction to the topic, raising awareness of the inside/outsider mentality many Christians unknowingly bring to the task of evangelism. It helps one understand what it's like to be lost physically and how to use that experience to better understand non-Christians. The last chapter is a review and practical application of some basic skills needed in sharing one's faith relationally. Chapters 2 through 5 each deal with six of the laws of lostology. They include reflection questions which call for a personal, emotional response as well as application questions which deal with more practical issues. After addressing each law, there is a lostology lab designed for small group discussion.

The 24 laws of lostology deal with two main topics. Laws 1-12 address those who are seeking direction while laws 13-24 shift to our role as Christians in searching for the lost. Chapter 2 (laws 1-6) helps us begin to understand what's going on with non-Christians before they begin their spiritual search. Chapter 3 (laws 7-12) looks at how the non-Christian begins to ask for spiritual directions and how we Christians give directions. Chapter 4 (laws 13-18) moves to our lives as spiritual searchers who can recognize when someone is lost and Chapter 5 (laws 19-24) offers practical suggestions for the searchers.

OUTLINE FOR TEACHING

1. BEGIN WITH PRAYER:
- •for participants
- •for leader
- •for clarity of thought
- •for understanding your own experience of lostness and how it can help you relate to spiritually lost people
- •for others who need to participate in a study of *Into Their Shoes*
- •for those you will encounter this week who may be asking for directions and for personal awareness of their searching

2. INTRODUCE THE CHAPTER TITLE AND TOPIC.

3. PRESENT THE CASE STUDY from the chapter introduction. Summarize the action or ask students to role-play. (Enlist appropriate actors for each week ahead of time.)

4. ASK FOR COMMENTS OR QUESTIONS from the personal studies which students have completed. If there are no questions, be prepared with one or two specific questions to stimulate discussion.

5. IN GROUPS OF 3-5, WORK THROUGH THE QUESTIONS in the lostology labs for the first five laws in the chapter. Share with the larger group if time allows.

6. ASK STUDENTS TO TACKLE ONE LAW PER DAY between group sessions because Chapters 2-5 are lengthy. Then, include the sixth law in each chapter as part of your group session.

7. FOCUS ON ONE OR TWO LAWS which highlight the chapter. (See suggestions which follow.)

8. CLOSE WITH PRAYER for openness, awareness, and development of relationships with those who are seeking direction in their lives.

CHAPTER 1
(The Lostology Experience, pages 8–15)
DISCUSSION SUGGESTIONS:
- What is your initial response to lostology? Do you think it will affect the way you relate to lost people?
- Have you ever considered before how you can relate to non-Christians by understanding shared experiences and emotions? by relating your physical experience of lostness with their spiritual experience?

CHAPTER 2
(You Can Learn A Lot By Being Lost, pages 16–35)
Focus on laws 4 and 5. This chapter looks at the experience of lost people and how easy it is to be lost whether you know it or admit it.
DISCUSSION SUGGESTIONS:
- Do you expect lost people to be open to hearing or talking about Jesus Christ?
- As you reflect on your own experiences of being physically lost and begin to understand how easy it is to be lost, how does this change the way you deal with lost people?
- What do you think causes non-Christians to take the first step toward acknowledging that they are not sure of their spiritual condition?
- In your personal experience with lost people, do they welcome the message that they are lost or do they resist it? Why?

CHAPTER 3
(When All Else Fails, Ask Directions, pages 36–59)
Focus on laws 8 and 9. This chapter deals with the emotional toll of being lost, the difficulty lost people face in finding themselves out of control.
DISCUSSION SUGGESTIONS:
- How do you attempt to compensate for your loss of control when you're lost?
- What do Christians do unintentionally that makes spiritual seekers feel more self-conscious or even stupid?
- Why is it important for Christians to work together and build relationships with non-Christians?
- What do you think are the most common mistakes direction-givers make which cause confusion?

CHAPTER 4
(The Cost of Being Lost, pages 60–81)

Focus on laws 13 and 17. A search always reveals our values; if we stop everything else in order to focus on a search, we obviously place great value on the lost item. If we choose not to search, the lost thing has little or no value to us ultimately. This chapter offers an eye-opening look at the Christian's personal motivation and involvement in evangelism and can be the beginning of a philosophical shift from fear of sharing one's faith with the lost to actively seeking the lost.

DISCUSSION SUGGESTIONS:

• Do you find that what you do in evangelism is sometimes inconsistent with the value you claim to place on lost people? How do you deal with this inconsistency?

• In what ways do we, as Christians, give the impression that we expect evangelism and outreach to be convenient and inexpensive?

• In what ways is evangelism costly?

• How do you deal with "acceptable loss" in relation to evangelism?

• Are you lost-centered or searcher-centered?

CHAPTER 5
(Secrets of a Successful Search, pages 82–103)

Focus on laws 23 and 24. This chapter offers practical advice about coordinating efforts and dealing with discouragement, but the highlight of this chapter is the good news that if you're searching, the lost may find you.

DISCUSSION SUGGESTIONS:

• Which is more important: each Christian sharing his faith or churches (groups, Sunday school classes, etc.) involved in outreach?

• How can you better handle discouragement?

• How can you make waiting active?

• What is your responsibility in evangelism?

• How does celebration reveal your values and priorities?

CHAPTER 6
(Your Life as a Lostologist, pages 104–113)

DISCUSSION SUGGESTIONS:

• How can you improve your testimony to include the crucial amount of information without including too much detail or more information than a non-Christian can easily handle?

• Are you comfortable using a prepared gospel presentation? Why or why not? What can you do to adapt a memorized presentation or printed tract so that it reveals more of your own walk with Christ?

• How do you plan to continue your study and your lifestyle as a "certified" lostologist?

NOTES